Lecture Notes in Computer Science 7303

Commenced Publication in 1973
Founding and Former Series Editors:
Gerhard Goos, Juris Hartmanis, and Jan van Leeuwen

Victor Pankratius   Michael Philippsen (Eds.)

Multicore Software Engineering, Performance, and Tools

International Conference, MSEPT 2012
Prague, Czech Republic, May 31 – June 1, 2012
Proceedings

 Springer

Volume Editors

Victor Pankratius
Karlsruhe Institute of Technology
Institute for Program Structures and Data Organization
Am Fasanengarten 5, b. 50.34, 76131 Karlsruhe, Germany
E-mail: pankratius@kit.edu

Michael Philippsen
Universität Erlangen-Nürnberg
Lehrstuhl für Programmiersysteme (Informatik 2)
Martensstr. 3, 91058 Erlangen, Germany
E-mail: philippsen@informatik.uni-erlangen.de

ISSN 0302-9743   e-ISSN 1611-3349
ISBN 978-3-642-31201-4   e-ISBN 978-3-642-31202-1
DOI 10.1007/978-3-642-31202-1
Springer Heidelberg Dordrecht London New York

Library of Congress Control Number: 2012939516

CR Subject Classification (1998): D.3.3, D.3.4, D.2.11, D.1.3, C.1.4, D.2.2, C.3, C.4, D.2, D.1.5, D.4.1

LNCS Sublibrary: SL 2 – Programming and Software Engineering

Typesetting: Camera-ready by author, data conversion by Scientific Publishing Services, Chennai, India

Printed on acid-free paper

Springer is part of Springer Science+Business Media (www.springer.com)

Preface

Welcome to MSEPT 2012, the International Conference on Multicore Software Engineering, Performance, and Tools. This conference emerged from the successful International Workshop on Multicore Software Engineering (IWMSE) series. IWMSE workshops were previously co-located with ICSE, the International Conference on Software Engineering, from 2008 to 2011.

The call for papers attracted 24 submissions by 63 authors from all over the world. In a double-blind review process, the Program Committee finally accepted nine papers, four of which are short papers. The accepted papers present new work on optimization of multicore software, program analysis, and automatic parallelization. In addition, these proceedings also provide new perspectives on programming models as well as on applications of multicore systems.

The MSEPT 2012 program also featured two excellent and well-known keynote speakers, Bertrand Meyer and Lionel Briand, who discussed the multicore programming challenges from a software engineering point of view.

We thank our Program Committee, the Organizing Committee of the co-located TOOLS conference, our authors, as well as the editorial team at Springer and everyone else who supported us to make MSEPT 2012 happen.

May 2012   Victor Pankratius
                                                          Michael Philippsen

Organization

Committees

Program Chairs

Victor Pankratius
Michael Philippsen

Program Committee

Siegfried Benkner
Koen De Bosschere
John Cavazos
Brian Demsky
Danny Dig
Eitan Farchi
Takahiro Katagiri

Christoph Kessler
Doug Lea
Raymond Namyst
Victor Pankratius
Michael Philippsen
Leonel Sousa
Richard Vuduc

Table of Contents

Keynotes

Papers

Processors and Their Collection

Bertrand Meyer[1,2,3], Alexander Kogtenkov[2,3], and Anton Akhi[3]

[1] ETH Zurich, Switzerland
[2] ITMO National Research University, Saint Petersburg, Russia
[3] Eiffel Software, Santa Barbara, California
se.ethz.ch, eiffel.com, sel.ifmo.ru

Abstract. In a flexible approach to concurrent computation, "processors" [1] (computational resources such as threads) are allocated dynamically, just as objects are; but then, just as objects, they can become unused, leading to performance degradation or worse. We generalized the notion of garbage collection (GC), traditionally applied to objects, so that it also handles collecting unused processors.

The paper describes the processor collection problem, formalizes it as a set of fixpoint equations, introduces the resulting objects-and-processor GC algorithm implemented as part of concurrency support (the SCOOP model) in the latest version of EiffelStudio, and presents benchmarks results showing that the new technique introduces no overhead as compared to traditional objects-only GC, and in fact improves its execution time slightly in some cases.

1   Overview

Few issues are more pressing today, in the entire field of information technology, than providing a safe and convenient way to program concurrent architectures. The SCOOP approach to concurrent computation [5] [6] [7] [8] [9], devised in its basic form as a small extension to Eiffel, is a comprehensive effort to make concurrent programming as understandable and reliable as traditional sequential programming. The model, whose basic ideas go back to the nineties, has been continuously refined and now benefits from a solid implementation integrated in the EiffelStudio environment.

One of the starting ideas of SCOOP, which it shares with some other concurrency models, is the notion of a "processor" as the basic unit of concurrency. A processor is a mechanism that can execute a sequence of instructions; it can concretely be implemented in many ways, either in hardware as a CPU, or in software as a single-threaded process or a thread.

When processors are implemented in software, they get created in a way similar to objects in object-oriented programming and, like objects, they may become inactive, raising a problem of garbage collection (GC). While object GC has been extensively studied (see [4] for a recent survey), we are not aware of previous discussions of processor GC, save for a discussion of a partly related problem for actors in [3]. What makes the problem delicate is that processor GC must be intricately connected with the classical *object* GC: to decide that a processor P is no longer useful and can

V. Pankratius and M. Philippsen (Eds.): MSEPT 2012, LNCS 7303, pp. 1–15, 2012.
© Springer-Verlag Berlin Heidelberg 2012

be collected, it is not enough to ascertain that P has no instructions left to execute; we must also make sure that no live object from another processor has a reference to an object handled by P and hence retains the possibility or soliciting P.

The present article discusses processor garbage collection as implemented in the latest release of EiffelStudio. It is not an introduction to SCOOP (which may be found in the references listed above) and indeed presents the concepts in a form that can be applied to many other concurrency models.

Section 2 explains the notion of processor as a general concurrency mechanism. Section 3 introduces the problem of collecting processors. Section 4 describes the constraints on any solution. Section 5 formalizes the problem as a set of two mutually recursive equations and introduces the resulting fixpoint algorithm. Section 6 presents the results of a number of benchmarks, showing no degradation and, in some case, performance improvements. Section 7 describes possibilities for future work.

The mechanism presented here has been fully implemented as part of the SCOOP implementation included in EiffelStudio version 7.1, available in both open-source and commercial licenses and downloadable from the Eiffel site [2] .

2   Processors

The concept of processor captures the basic difference between sequential and concurrent computation: in sequential mode, there is only one mechanism capable of executing instructions one after the other; in concurrent mode, we may combine several such mechanisms. The problems of concurrency arise out of the need to coordinate these individual sequential computations.

2.1   Handlers and Regions

This definition of processors would be close to a platitude — concurrent computation is concurrent because it can pursue several sequential tasks at once — were it not for the connection with object-oriented programming as established in SCOOP: the assignment of every *object* to a single processor. Object-oriented computation is dominated by the basic operation

$$x.f\,(args)$$

a *feature call* (also called "method call" and "message passing"), which applies a feature (operation) f to an object x, the **target** of the call, with some optional arguments *args*. Concurrent mechanisms that have not been specifically designed for the object-oriented paradigm, such as Java Threads, enforce no particular connection between the concurrency structure (the division into processors) and the object structure; the standard risks of concurrent programming, in particular data races, arise as a result, and can only be avoided through programmer discipline such as the use of "synchronized" calls. SCOOP makes the connection between the processor and object structures by assigning, for every object **O**, a single processor — the object's **handler** — to execute all calls having **O** as their target. Since processors are sequential, this decision also means that at most one operation may be proceeding on any given target object at any given time (although compiler optimization may produce exceptions to this rule as long as they preserve the semantics).

The practical consequence of this policy is a partition of the object space in one-to-one correspondence with the set of processors:

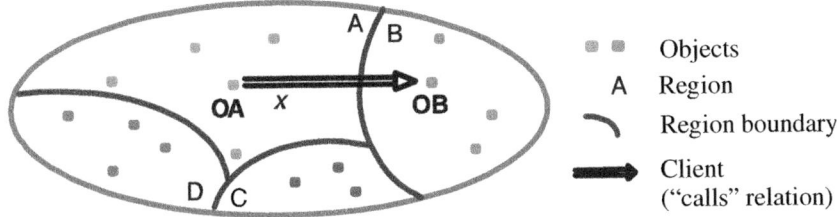

Fig. 1. Processors cause a partition of objects into regions

Each element of the partition, containing all the objects handled by a particular processor, is called a **region**.

In the figure, a call may be executed on behalf of the object **OA**, and hence as part of a computation performed by its handler, the processor A; since the call has the target x denoting the object **OB**, handled by another processor B, it will be executed by B.

A call handled by a different processor, as here since the call starts from A but is executed by B on its behalf, calls for appropriate semantics; specifically in SCOOP, the call is:

- **Asynchronous** if the feature is a command (a procedure, executing some actions), since there is no need in this case for A to wait; if it did, there would be no benefit from concurrency.
- **Synchronous** if it is a query (a function computing a result, or a lookup of a value in a field) since in this case the result is needed for the computation to proceed. This is the mechanism of wait by necessity [1] [5] .

To make this specific behavior clear, programmers must declare **separate** (the only new Eiffel keyword for SCOOP) a variable such as x to specify that it may denote objects handled by a processor other than the current object's handler. Such a declaration does not specify the processor; it simply states that this processor may be different, and hence lead to a different semantics for calls. The SCOOP type system [8] guarantees semantic consistency; in particular it is not permitted to assign from separate to non-separate.

2.2   Call vs. Application

One of the consequences of treating command calls with a separate target as asynchronous is to introduce a refinement of the classical notion of feature call $x.f$ (*args*). In a concurrent context we must distinguish between the feature's *call* and its *application*:

- The calling processor (A in the earlier figure) executes a call. If the call is asynchronous, the processor does not wait and proceeds to its next instruction. At the implementation level, the only needed operation is to **log** the call with the supplier processor, which typically uses a queue to record such logged requests).
- At some later time, the supplier processor (B in the figure) will be ready to execute the call's instruction. This is the actual **application** of the feature.

This separation between call and application is the defining property of asynchrony as permitted by concurrent computation.

2.3   Call Logging

Every processor may log several separate calls to different processors. One way to implement processors is to set up each of them as a loop that looks at the queue of logged calls, retrieves one call, and applies it. It is not possible to determine automatically when to terminate this loop (any more than to solve any other general termination problem). We may note, however, that a processor is no longer useful when:

- No calls are logged on it (at the implementation level, its queue is empty).
- No object from another (live) processor contains a reference to one of its own objects.

Note that the second condition does not imply the first: even though the client processor A that executed $x.f\,(args)$ had a reference — namely, x — to an object **OB** of the supplier processor B at the time of the call, A may not be keeping any direct interest in the result of the call; the operation that executed $x.f\,(args)$ may itself have terminated and the object **OA** that contained it may have been reclaimed. It is still obligated, however, to execute the logged operation.

3   Collecting Processors

We will now review the issues raised by extending traditional garbage collection to a concurrent environment.

3.1   The Need for Processor Garbage Collection

For general discussions of concurrency, and for writing concurrent programs, it does not matter how the processors are physically implemented; the general definition that a processor is a mechanism capable of executing instructions sequentially suffices. In the context of the present discussion a processor is a software mechanism; in the current EiffelStudio implementation, processors are indeed implemented as threads, although future versions may provide other representations, particularly in a distributed context.

Concretely, a processor gets created every time a creation instruction (equivalent to a "new" in C++/Java syntax) is executed with a separate target:

> **create** *x* .*make* (...)-- With *x* : **separate** *T* for some typed *T*.
>   -- *make* is the creation procedure (constructor).

(Here too compilers optimizations may avoid the creation of a new physical resource, for example the implementation may reuse an existing thread, but conceptually the instruction creates a new processor.)

Since processors are allocated dynamically, the same problem arises as with objects in ordinary object-oriented programming languages supporting dynamic object allocation (such as Java, Eiffel or C#): some processors may become unused; if not reclaimed, they will waste resources, and possibly lead to resource exhaustion and program freezing. For example an inactive thread takes up space to hold its local data, and takes up CPU time if the thread scheduler continues to examine it. As with objects, it may be desirable to reclaim — garbage-collect — unused processors.

3.2   Challenges of Processor GC

Object garbage collection is a classic research topic with an abundant literature, which we will not attempt to review, referring the reader instead to [4] . To what extent can the concepts apply to processor GC?

Any garbage collection mechanism, whether for objects or for some other resource, conceptually includes two aspects: *detection*, which identifies unused resources, and *reclamation*, which frees them or recycles them for new needs. Typical schemes such as "mark-and-sweep" refine this idea: the mark phase implements detection by traversing the object structure, starting from a set of root objects known to be alive and recursively following all references to flag all the objects it reaches; the sweep phase implements reclamation by traversing all memory and reclaiming all unmarked objects (as well as unmarking all objects in preparation for the next GC cycle).

In trying to transpose these concepts to processor collection, the principal issue is that it is not sufficient, for detection, to determine that a processor has no more instructions of its own to execute: another condition, already noted in 2.3 , is that *none of its objects has an incoming reference from an object handled by another processor*. Were such a reference to exist, it could later on cause a new request for computation if the other processor is itself (recursively) still active. This specification is sufficiently delicate to require a formal specification, to be given in section 5.3 .

4   Practical Requirements on an Objects+Processors GC

An effective solution to processor collection must take into account a number of practical issues.

4.1   Triggering Conditions

In classical object GC, the trigger for a collection cycle is typically that memory usage has gone beyond a certain threshold.

The concurrent GC scheme adds another threshold, on the number of processors. If processors have been allocated beyond that threshold, the GC will be triggered to reclaim any unused processors.

4.2   Root Objects

The need to take object references into account shows that the mechanisms of object GC and processor GC are not independent, but mutually recursive. In line with this observation, the algorithm that we have implemented integrates processor GC within the preexisting object GC algorithm, maintaining a queue of active processors initialized with the processors known to be active (the processors that still have instructions to execute) and enriching it, during object traversals, with the processors handling objects that are found to be reachable.

The concurrent setup introduces one more issue not present in sequential GC: root objects. All GC algorithms need to start from a set (the *root set*) of objects known for sure to be alive (the *root objects*). The first complication is that we must deal not with a single root set but with a multiplicity of root sets, one per processor. Another issue arises in the case of global objects; in the Eiffel context these are the result of "once functions" (functions that, as the name implies, are executed — "applied" in the earlier terminology — only once, upon their first call, with the result saved and returned in any subsequent call). In another language, static variables would raise a similar difficulty. If there are no references from other processors to the result of a once function, the basic algorithm just outlined would collect it; this behavior is clearly unsound, but the solution of treating all such objects as roots is also unsatisfactory as they would then never be collected even though some of them may not be live.

4.3   Memory Overhead

Taking processors into account requires supplementary memory structures. In particular it is necessary to record a "processor ID" for any object, identifying the object's handler. Fortunately, we were able in EiffelStudio's internal representation of objectsto reuse two heretofore available bytes. As a consequence, the memory overhead is zero.

4.4   Time Overhead

A straightforward extension to conventional object GC would handle every processor as if it were an object. Such a special processor object would contain references to the objects in its root set and, conversely, every object would have an implicit reference to the processor object corresponding to its processor ID.

This solution introduces an overhead since it adds a conceptual reference to every object. The benchmarks (see section 6.4) confirm that the overhead would be significant. The algorithm described below avoids it by separating the objects and the processors. In addition:

- The overhead during object traversal consists of a single unconditional write that can be efficiently handled by the out-of-order instruction execution available on today's CPUs.
- All the memory used to track live processors is allocated in a very small contiguous chunk that fits the CPU cache; this technique avoids cache misses and reduces the write time to the minimum.
- The most expensive traversal part associated with the root sets of the processors is executed separately.

The result of these optimizations, confirmed by the benchmarks of section 6 , is that the implementation avoids any significant slowdown as compared to the non-concurrent GC collecting objects only, and in fact slightly improves the performance in some cases.

4.5   Object Revival

Many GC-enabled languages and environments offer the possibility of associating with objects of a certain type a "finalization" routine (in Eiffel, *dispose* from the library class *DISPOSABLE*) which will be called whenever a GC cycle reaches one of these objects, say A, considered dead. In the absence of any restriction, such a mechanism threatens the soundness and completeness of the garbage collector:

- Although A has been marked as dead (ready for collection), the finalization routine could add a reference to A from some other object B that is live, reviving A and preventing its collection.
- The routine could execute a call *x.f* (...) using a reference *x* in A, but the corresponding object C might be dead.

In a concurrent setting the referenced objects could have a different handler, so finalization could cause the revival of a processor.

Because of these problems, the Eiffel environment enforces a strong restriction on finalization routines, both in a sequential setting and in SCOOP: such a routine may not include any qualified call (that is to say, any call *x.f* (...) with an explicit target *x*). Unqualified calls (*f* (...), applying to the current object) are permitted.

4.6   Partial GC

Modern "generational" object GC systems support partial garbage collection, which reclaims some objects without traversing the entire heap. The EiffelStudio implementation performs frequent partial collection, which minimizes the performance impact on the computation, and occasional full collection, to reclaim any dead objects that the partial GC cycles did not detect.

As will be detailed below, object GC in a concurrent context mutually depends on processor GC. We have not yet found a way to integrate this double GC mechanism in the partial collection algorithm. As a consequence, processor GC only occurs during the full collection cycles.

5   Devising an Objects+Processors GC Problem

We now describe the GC design, starting with an informal description of the problem and continuing with a mathematical description and a presentation of the algorithm.

5.1   Root Sets

As noted in 4.2, the starting point of any GC process is the root set. In a concurrent setting the root set contains two parts:

- A set of *system-wide root objects*, not related to any processor.
- For each live processor, a set of *processor-specific root objects*.

The precise definition of liveness for processors appears next (5.2).

The second part, processor-specific root objects, includes for each processor: objects on its call stack; objects on its evaluation stack (when the implementation uses interpreted code); objects on other run-time stacks (in the presence of calls to external software, as supported for example by Eiffel's C/C++ interface); results of processor-level once functions; activation records containing the targets and arguments of separate feature calls.

As specified, we need only consider the processor-specific root object sets of *live* processors. This property causes a modification of the object GC algorithm: instead of starting from all potential root objects it can restrict itself to live processors.

5.2   When Is a Processor Ready for Collection?

To determine when processors are "live" and "dead", we note that the typical steps in the life of a processor are the following:

- On processor creation, logging a call to a creation procedure (constructor, such as *make* in the instruction **create** *x.make* (...) where *x* is separate, which creates a new object on a new processor and initializes the object through *make*).
- As a result of a call from another processor, logging a separate feature call.
- If the log queue contains a call ready for application, removing it from the queue and applying the feature.

A processor is dead when it cannot perform any useful work, right now or in the future. This is the case when both:

- It has no currently logged calls.
- No calls can ever be logged in the future.

The first condition is local to the processor; the second one involves the entire system. This second condition, however, is undecidable. We need a stronger condition that can be checked; that condition is that the processor's objects are not reachable through references from live objects (from any processors). It is clearly stronger than needed, since we do not know that such references will ever be followed, but it is sound. Hence the definition of liveness that we retain for practical purposes:

Definition: dead, live processor

A processor is **dead** if both:

1 It has no calls logged and not yet applied.

2 None of its objects is referenced by a live object.

A processor is **live** if it is not dead.

The set of live objects, necessary for the second part of the definition, is obtained by traversal of the object structure starting from the root set. We have just seen, however, that the root set includes the processor-specific root sets of live processors. As a consequence, the definitions of liveness for objects and processors are mutually recursive; they will now be formalized.

5.3   Formal Description

We may describe the processor collection object mathematically as follows. The two sets of interest are LO, the set of live objects, and LP, the set of live processors. They will be defined by a set of two mutually recursive equations.

We assume a set BP (for "basic processors") of processors known to be live — as their log queues are not empty — and a set BR ("basic roots") of objects known to be live.

The function h (for "handler") maps objects to their processors. We will write $h\,(o)$ not only when o denotes a single object but also when it denotes a set of objects, the result then being a set of processors. In other words we use the same name h for the handler function and the associated image function.

For a processor p, $r\,(p)$ (r for "roots") denotes the set of its root objects. As in the previous case, r will also be applied to sets of processors; $r\,(P)$, for a set P of processors, denotes the union of the individual root sets of the processors in P.

The set of objects to which an object o contains references (links) is written $s\,(o)$ (s for "successors"), again generalized to sets of objects. As usual, * denotes reflexive transitive closure, so that the set of objects reachable from the objects in a set O is $s^*(O)$.

The sets LO and LP of live objects and processors depend on each other and on the reference structure, as defined by the following equations:

$$
\begin{aligned}
LO &= s^*\,(BR \cup r\,(LP)) & &/1/ \\
LP &= BP \cup h\,(LO) & &/2/
\end{aligned}
$$

5.4   Algorithm

$/1/$ and $/2/$ is a fixpoint equation of the form $f = \tau\,(f)$ on functions f applying to $[LO, LP]$ pairs. We are looking for a minimum fixpoint (with respect to the partial order defined by set inclusion, generalized to [*objects, processors*] subset pairs), since we should only retain objects and processors that are strictly necessary, and reclaim any others. The function τ is monotonic; since the underlying sets of objects and processors are finite, fixpoint theory tells us that a minimal fixpoint exists and can be obtained as the finitely reached limit of the sequences LO_i and LP_i defined as follows:

$$LO_0 = BR \qquad\qquad /3/$$
$$LP_0 = BP \qquad\qquad /4/$$
$$LO_{i+1} = s\,(LO_i \cup r\,(LP_i)) \qquad\qquad /5/$$
$$LP_{i+1} = LP_i \cup h\,(LO_i) \qquad\qquad /6/$$

which readily yields the basic algorithm:

```
from                                                              /7/
     LO := BR ; LP := BP              -- done initialized to False
until
     done
loop
     saved_LO := LO
     LO := s (LO ∪ r (LP))
     LP := LP ∪ h (saved_LO)
     done := "No change to LO and LP since last iteration"
end
```

The algorithm is guaranteed to terminate as a consequence of the preceding observations. In practice we can do away with *saved_LO* since the algorithm remains sound if we replace the body of the loop by just

```
     LO := s (LO ∪ r (LP))
     LP := LP ∪ h (LO)
     done := "No change to LO and LP since last iteration"
```

The algorithm can be further improved by computing at each step the difference between the new and old values of LO and LP, rather than recomputing the whole sets each time. /7/ with these two improvements (for the details of the implementation, the reader can refer to the open-source code available from [2]) is the basic algorithm for combined object-processor collection, as has been implemented in EiffelStudio 7.1.

6   Performance Evaluation

To evaluate the performance, we wrote three test programs that allocate up to 10 million objects and use up to 100 processors. Calculations have been performed on a computer with a 3.2GHz AMD Phenom II processor and 4GB of RAM.

The first test involves independent data structures, each local to a processor; the next ones use structures that are distributed among processors.

6.1   Test Setup

Each test proceeded through the following procedure, repeated fifty times with the results then averaged:

- Turn off garbage collection (through the corresponding mechanisms in the Eiffel libraries).
- Create object structures.
- Explicitly trigger a full garbage collection (again through a library mechanism).

6.2   Test Results

The first test is intended to assess the basic overhead of adding processor GC to object GC, in the case of independent data structures. It creates full binary tree structures, with various heights, on different processors. All the nodes in each tree have the same handler, so that garbage collection could be performed almost independently on different processors.

Figure 2 shows the time dependency on number of processors for two tree depths. Numbers of objects in this figure and the following ones are in thousands.

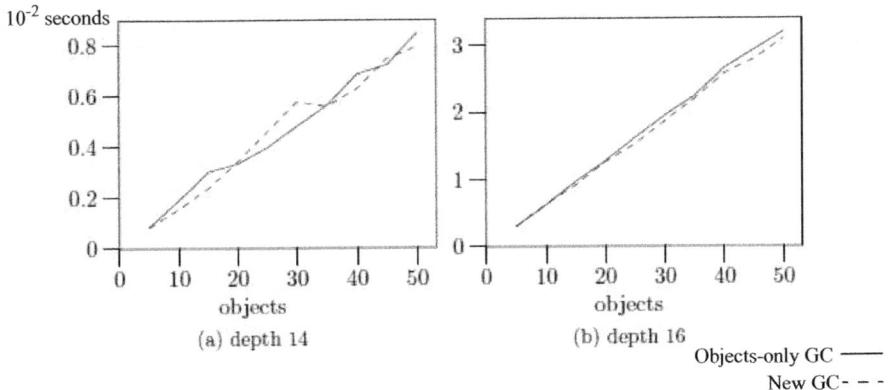

Fig. 2. Processor-specific binary trees

The second test consists of cyclic structures, with nodes randomly allocated to processors; it is intended to measure the GC algorithm's ability to move from processor to processor during the marking phase, and to collect structures with cyclic links. Figure 3 shows the time dependency on the number of processors ((a) and (b)) and objects ((c) and (d)).

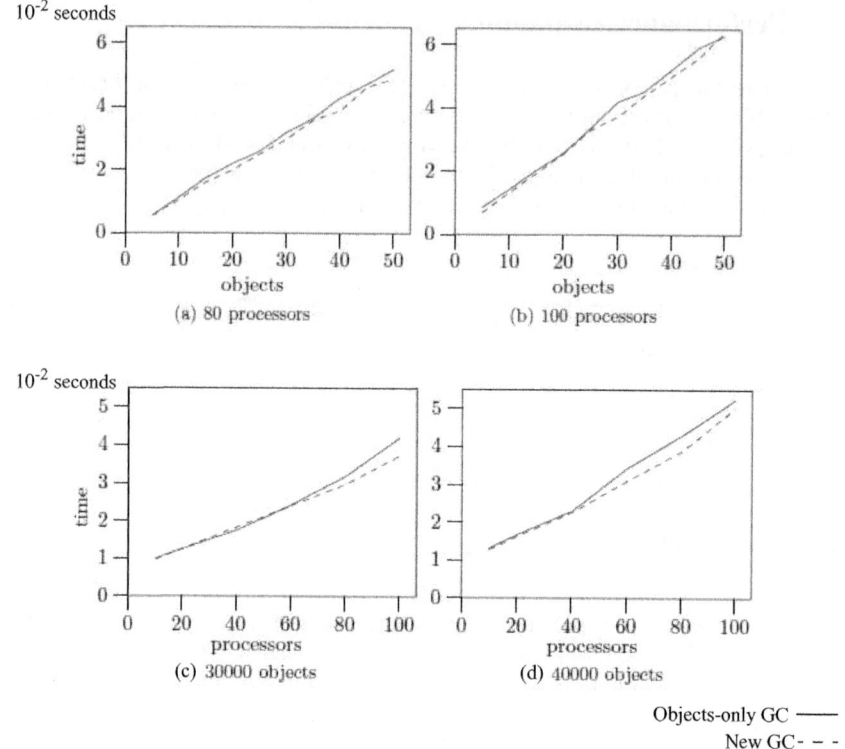

Fig. 3. Randomly distributed cyclic structures

The next test randomly creates objects on processors. From each object, up to ten random links to other objects were created. Because of the large number of objects, their spread across processors, and the large number of links, this test yields many interesting cases for the algorithm. Figure 4 shows the outcome.

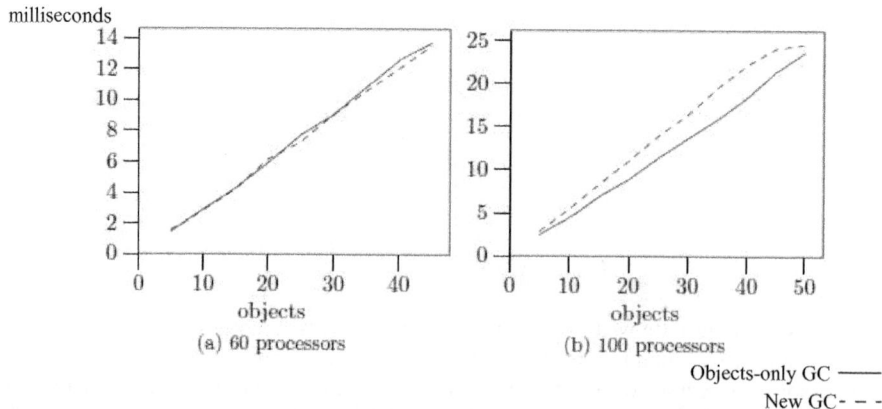

Fig. 4. Random processor allocation and numerous links

6.3   Assessment

The results shown above indicate that in general the new algorithm's execution time remains essentially the same as that of the previous, objects-only GC.

In some cases the new algorithm is actually faster. Several factors may explain this improvement:

- The new algorithm does not need to perform marking of objects on dead processors.
- Since it only traverses objects from live processors, there is a good chance that some of those objects were recently used by program and are available in the processor's cache. The previous algorithm could cause loads from memory in such cases.
- The new algorithm visits objects in a different order, which may have some effects on the performance.

6.4   Assessing the Processor-as-Object Approach

We added a test to compare the proposed algorithm and the straightforward approach of treating processors simply as objects, discussed in section 4.4 . The test emulates the resulting overhead by adding a reference field to every object. Figure 5 shows the comparison with the algorithm without such reference fields.

For practical reasons, the reference field has been added in both versions; it is simply void (null) in the "new GC" version. Although this technique introduces a small difference with the real algorithm, we believe that any resulting bias is very small (and probably to the detriment of the new algorithm).

The results of the test clearly show an overhead of 6% to 12% for the processors-as-objects approach. This overhead linearly increases with the number of objects, whereas there is no noticeable increase with the retained algorithm.

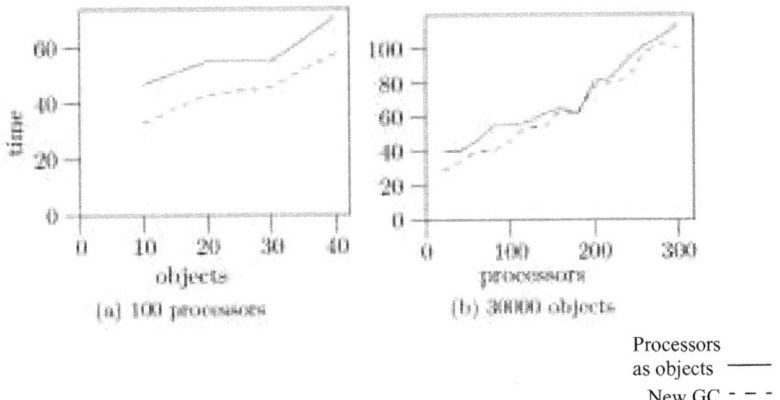

Fig. 5. Overhead of treating processors as objects

7   Other Applications and Future Work

As noted, the problem address in this article, garbage-collecting processors, is essentially new. The work reported here has shown that an efficient and sound solution is possible. The key idea is to treat object GC and processor GC as intricately (and recursively) connected, modeling and performing them together.

While implemented for Eiffel and SCOOP, the algorithm relies only on the properties listed in this article, in particular the notion of processor; it is independent of many characteristics of a programming language, such as its type system, and is therefore of potential application to different models of concurrency.

Some of the highlights of the approach are that:

- Memory is not shared but distributed among execution resources.
- The algorithm makes it possible to provide information about active resources.
- At presents it only works in the context of a full GC cycles.
- There is a reachability function for memory resources.

The last requirement does not assume fine-grained resolution: it is sufficient to work on the level of memory regions belonging to the specific execution flow. The approach discussed here does use object-level information to collect unused processors, but only to demonstrate that this scheme can be naturally integrated with the existing traditional GC. This leads us to assume that the algorithm can be applied in a completely distributed setting, but we have not yet examined this extension (including support for fault tolerance) in detail.

An important topic for further research is automatic management of reclaimed execution resources. In this paper we intentionally left out the details about acquiring and releasing resources from the underlying operating environment. In some systems where these operations are costly, it may make sense to preallocate pools of execution resources and apply load balancing, to allow efficient operation in highly dynamic conditions.

Acknowledgments. The implementation described here is part of the SCOOP mechanism of EiffelStudio, developed at Eiffel Software, to which key other contributors are Emmanuel Stapf and Ian King. The benefit of discussions with members of the SCOOP team at ETH Zurich, in particular Sebastian Nanz, Benjamin Morandi and Scott West, is gratefully acknowledged.

We are greatly indebted to the funding agencies that have made the work on SCOOP possible. The SCOOP project at ETH has been supported by grants from the Swiss National Science Foundation and the Hasler foundation, an ETH ETHIIRA grant, and a Multicore Award from Microsoft Research. The ITMO Software Engineering Laboratory is supported by a grant from Mail.ru group.

References

[1] Caromel, D.: Towards A Method of Object-Oriented Concurrent Programming. Communications of the ACM 36(9), 90–102 (1993)
[2] EiffelStudio environment, available for download at http://eiffel.com

[3] Kafura, D., Washabaugh, D., Nelson, J.: Garbage collection of actors. In: OOPSLA/ECOOP 1990, pp. 126–134 (1990)

[4] Jones, R., Hosking, A., Moss, E.: The Garbage Collection Handbook: The Art of Automatic Memory Management, 2nd edn. Chapman and Hall/CRC (2011)

[5] Meyer, B.: Systematic Concurrent Object-Oriented Programming. Communications of the ACM 36(9), 56–80 (1993)

[6] Meyer, B.: Object-Oriented Software Construction, 2nd edn. Prentice Hall (1997) (chapter 32 presents SCOOP)

[7] Morandi, B., Nanz, S., Meyer, B.: A Formal Reference for SCOOP. In: Meyer, B., Nordio, M. (eds.) LASER Summer School 2008-2010. LNCS, vol. 7007, pp. 89–157. Springer, Heidelberg (2012)

[8] Nienaltowski, P.: Practical framework for contract-based concurrent object-oriented programming. PhD dissertation 17061, Department of Computer Science, ETH Zurich (February 2007), http://se.ethz.ch/old/people/nienaltowski/papers/thesis.pdf

[9] Nienaltowski, P., Ostroff, J., Meyer, B.: Contracts for Concurrency. Formal Aspects of Computing Journal 21(4), 305–318 (2009)

[10] Wilson, P.R.: Uniprocessor Garbage Collection Techniques. In: Bekkers, Y., Cohen, J. (eds.) IWMM-GIAE 1992. LNCS, vol. 637, pp. 1–42. Springer, Heidelberg (1992)

Tackling the Testing and Verification of Multicore and Concurrent Software as a Search Problem

Lionel C. Briand

Centre for Security, Reliability, and Trust (SnT), University of Luxembourg,
Luxembourg
lionel.briand@uni.lu

Keynote Abstract

As multicore and therefore concurrent architectures are spreading to an increasing number of applications and industry sectors, it becomes increasingly important to devise rigorous but practical ways to verify and test concurrent systems. Though a great deal of research work has been published on the matter, there is limited support in industry for the practicing engineer. For a change in engineering practice to happen, we need to devise technologies that scale and can be easily tailored to resources available for quality assurance in a given context.

This talk reports on a research program that approaches verification and testing as a search and optimization problem. The techniques presented rely on system models describing the task architecture and performance characteristics. As a strategy to ease adoption in practice, those models rely on standards (e.g., UML/MARTE) or lightweight extensions enabling the use of commercial or open source modeling platforms to support automation. Once the required in-formation is extracted from models, early verification and testing both consist in identifying scenarios that maximize chances of uncovering concurrency and performance issues, such as deadline misses, starvation, or unacceptable levels of CPU usage. To do so, we either rely on evolutionary computation or constraint optimization, for which effective support already exists. The main challenge is of course to transform each specific problem into a search or constraint optimization problem, in such a way that these technologies can be efficient and scale.

Short Biography

Lionel C. Briand is professor and FNR PEARL chair in software verification and validation at the SnT centre for Security, Reliability, and Trust, University of Luxembourg. Lionel started his career as a software engineer and has conducted applied research in collaboration with industry for more than 20 years.

Until moving to Luxembourg in January 2012, he was heading the Certus center for software verification and validation at Simula Research Laboratory,

V. Pankratius and M. Philippsen (Eds.): MSEPT 2012, LNCS 7303, pp. 16–17, 2012.

where he was leading applied re-search projects in collaboration with industrial partners. Before that, he was on the faculty of the department of Systems and Computer Engineering, Carleton University, Ottawa, Canada, where he was full professor and held the Canada Research Chair (Tier I) in Software Quality Engineering. He has also been the software quality engineering department head at the Fraun-hofer Institute for Experimental Software Engineering, Germany, and worked as a research scientist for the Software Engineering Laboratory, a consortium of the NASA Goddard Space Flight Center, CSC, and the University of Maryland, USA.

Lionel was elevated to the grade of IEEE Fellow for his work on the testing of object-oriented systems. He was recently granted the IEEE Computer Society Harlan Mills award for his work on model-based verification and testing.

Oversubscription of Computational Resources on Multicore Desktop Systems

Constantin Christmann[1], Erik Hebisch[1], and Anette Weisbecker[2]

[1] Universität Stuttgart,
Institut für Arbeitswissenschaft und Technologiemanagement,
Nobelstr. 12, 70569 Stuttgart, Germany
[2] Fraunhofer-Institut für Arbeitswirtschaft und Organisation IAO,
Nobelstr. 12 70569 Stuttgart, Germany

Abstract. The increasing pervasiveness of multicore processors in to-day's computing systems will increase the demand for techniques to adapt application level parallelism. In this paper we demonstrate the impact of oversubscription in the context of a desktop scenario and show that using too many threads in one application can lead to significant performance loss for other applications within the system environment (in our example more than 30%). We examine how common parallelization tools are trying to exploit parallelism while not causing oversubscription and find that common tools do not offer a mechanism which sufficiently takes into account the computational load of the system. Oversubscription is not easy to detect from an application perspective due to the fair scheduling of common operating systems. Nonetheless, we do present an approach for detecting oversubscription by exploiting a scheduling artifact in the average execution time of a parallel code section.

Keywords: oversubscription, multicore processors, desktop environment, parallelization.

1 Introduction

The increasing pervasiveness of multicore processors in today's computing systems, from clusters, over ordinary desktop computers, to mobile devices and embedded systems, will increase the demand for techniques to adapt application level parallelism. On a Shared Memory Processor (SMP) parallelism is generally achieved via threading. In the threading approach multiple threads are used for the processing of individual tasks of a parallel section. The scheduling of these threads onto actual processing elements (PE), like physical threads or processor cores, is then generally managed by the operating system.

The number of threads used within a parallel code section is an important aspect for good parallel performance. The optimal number of threads depends on the resources being consumed within the individual tasks of the parallel section. Such resources are commonly computational resources, like CPUs and memory, but they could as well be requests to a database or file I/O. In this work we focus on the consumption of computational resources alone.

V. Pankratius and M. Philippsen (Eds.): MSEPT 2012, LNCS 7303, pp. 18–29, 2012.

When there are not enough running threads to optimally exploit available PEs undersubscription occurs, resulting in a waste of performance. On the other hand, if more threads are used than PEs available, this causes oversubscription, which results in performance loss due to scheduling effects like context switching or cache cooling [1].

In the world of High Performance Computing (HPC) normally a parallel application is running alone on a single compute node. The system is approximately idle and the parallel application can utilize all computational resources available. In contrast to that, this work focuses on the desktop scenario, where multiple equally important applications may be running concurrently within the same system environment. In such competitive setting all applications share the computational resources based on a specific scheduling scheme.

The remainder of this paper is structured as follows: in Sect. 2 we demonstrate the impact of oversubscription in the context of a simple desktop scenario. In Sect. 3 we examine how common parallelization tools are trying to exploit parallelism while not causing oversubscription. In Sect. 4 we present an approach for detecting oversubscription by exploiting a scheduling artifact in the average execution time of a parallel code section. Section 5 presents related work and Sect. 6 concludes with a discussion and an outlook on further research opportunities.

2   Impact of Oversubscription

In order to see how the number of utilized threads affects other applications running within the same system environment we conducted a simple experiment. The execution environment was a Dual Clovertown (2.33 GHz, 64 bit) with 8 cores and Windows 7 running as operating system. Our test application was a matrix multiplication, where the outer-most loop has been parallelized using Intel Threaded Building Blocks (TBB). The number of threads of the TBB worker pool was explicitly set.

Two instances of this test application were executed concurrently. The first instance (application A) used a varying number of threads $x \in \{1, ..., 2N\}$, N being the number of available PEs on the machine. The second instance (application B) was always using a fixed number of 4 threads for its computations. We now measured the execution times for the parallel code sections of both applications A and B, based on the number of threads used in application A. Multiple trials for every x were performed in order to compute the average execution time.

Figure 1 shows the average execution time of each application, A and B, depending on the number of threads used for the parallel section of application A. At $x > 4$ a system wide oversubscription is occurring due to the fact that the number of busy threads of both applications is greater than the number of available PEs. As a result the execution time of B is significantly getting worse.

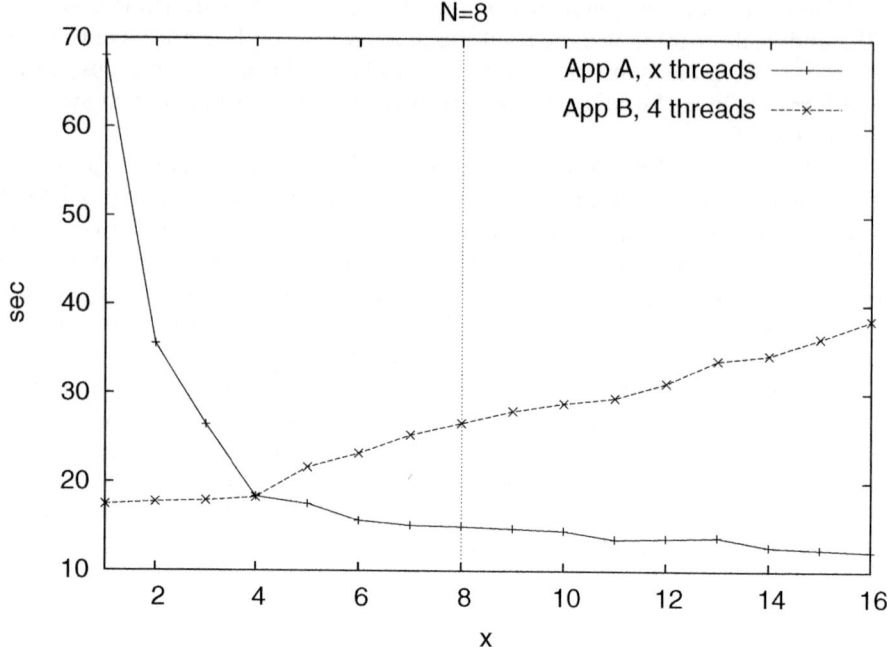

Fig. 1. Visualization of the average execution time of application A and B, depending on the number of threads used for the parallel section of application A

Interestingly this is not the case for application A. The execution time of A is getting better even when the system is clearly overloaded. It even improves if application A alone uses more threads than PEs available ($x > 8$).

The reason for this is that the thread scheduler of the operating system typically distributes time slices in a round-robin fashion. This distribution is called "fair", because each thread gets its fair share of time [1]. So in case of an oversubscription each of these threads gets an equal partition of the available computational resources.

To be more precise, let application A be utilizing x threads and let application B be using r threads for its computation ($x, r \in \mathbb{N}$, $x > 0$, $r \geq 0$). Let all $r + x$ threads be of the same priority and always ready to run, which means they are never in a waiting state due to synchronization or I/O. Let both applications be executed in a system environment with N PEs, $N \in \mathbb{N}$, $N > 0$. In case of an oversubscription ($r + x > N$) the available resources are fairly distributed among all $r + x$ threads, so the partition of computational resource application A gets can be estimated as

$$p(x) := \frac{x}{r + x} \ . \tag{1}$$

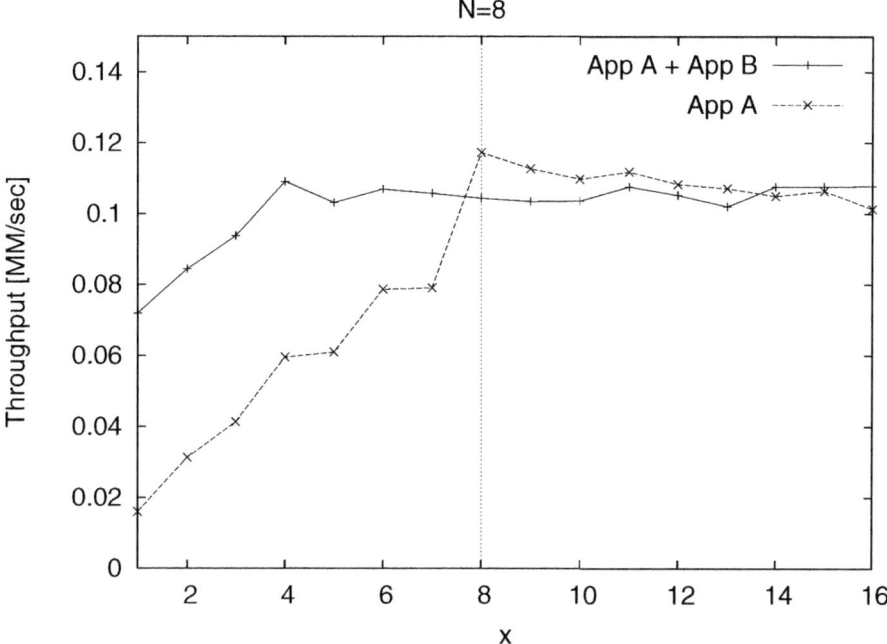

Fig. 2. The solid line shows the average throughput of both applications A and B. The dashed line visualizes the throughput of application A if it is running alone on the system.

As this quotient is approaching 1 for growing x (with r kept constant) application A is getting an increasing partition of the computational resources. As a result the computation of A is more and more superimposing the calculations of other applications within the system environment. Due to the fair thread scheduling policy it is hard for an application to prevent such oversubscription from happening just by looking at its own parallel throughput. As we see the throughput may be always improving even when the system is clearly overloaded.

Figure 2 shows the average throughput of the whole system environment. This throughput is computed as the number of matrix multiplications per second of both applications A and B (the solid line) or just application A alone on an idle system (the dashed line). In both cases the overall throughput is maximal if the number of threads $r + x$ meets the number of available PEs. As soon as this limit is exceeded the overall throughput stays constant or even decreases to a small percentage due to the scheduling overhead and context switching.

In this paper we focus on computational resources alone, however the described effect may be observable for other system resources too, if they also become distributed to individual threads in a round-robin fashion.

3   Common Tools

We have looked at popular parallelization tools in order to find out how they try to exploit available PEs optimally and if they offer a mechanism to prevent an oversubscription:

- Intel Threaded Building Blocks (TBB): The Intel TBB library uses the concept of tasks which become assigned to logical threads. It uses exactly one logical thread per physical thread (here PE) for the processing of these tasks. Within Intel TBB a scheduler is responsible for the load-balancing between logical threads in order to keep all physical threads busy [1].

  As the Intel TBB library allocates one logical thread per PE an oversubscription of an otherwise idle system cannot happen. However, the Intel TBB library does not contain a mechanism to dynamically adjust the utilization of its logical threads based on a varying computational load.

- OpenMP: For a parallel section OpenMP normally uses as many threads as PEs available, which just prevents oversubscription of an otherwise idle system. In order to react to varying computational load the specification of OpenMP describes the environmental variable OMP_DYNAMIC. When enabled, the number of threads used within a parallel section is dynamically chosen in order to optimize the use of system resources [2]. The actual algorithm behind this decision is left to the implementation.

  We looked at the gcc implementation of OpenMP (GOMP)[1] and the heuristic it uses is the following: first it calls the function getloadavg(), which returns the average number of running processes of the last few minutes. GOMP then uses this number to set the number of threads of a parallel section as the difference between the number of available cores and this average number of running processes. As the comment in the source code suggests, this is a very raw heuristic and it is likely to fail if other processes are using more than one thread for their computations.

- .NET Common Language Runtime (CLR): In recent versions the CLR worker thread pool has been subject to major changes regarding its mechanism to find the optimal number of threads actively doing work. The approaches ranged from optimization based on CPU utilization, over a hill climbing algorithm, to signal processing techniques in its latest release 4.0.

  This signal processing approach uses a constantly varying number of threads as an input signal and measures if and how the input variation affects the parallel throughput (output). Doing this the CLR is able to maximize the parallel throughput while avoiding oversubscription if the system load changes over time. However, the optimization function focuses on maximizing the application's throughput, not the global throughput of the whole system environment [3].

Regarding the prevention of oversubscription Intel TBB and OpenMP do only use very raw heuristics. The gcc implementation of OpenMP at least tries to

---

[1] SVN checkout (09-16-2010), libgomp/config/linux/proc.c

adapt its thread utilization based on a system wide load situation. The CLR automatically tackles oversubscription as well as undersubscription using an adaptive signal processing mechanism. However, it does not take into account the whole system environment as it realizes only a local optimization of the application's throughput. None of the examined parallelization tools offers an effective mechanism which takes into account the computational load of the system as a whole. As demonstrated in section 2, this can lead to significant performance loss for other applications executed within the same environment.

4 Detecting Oversubscription

As described before, in a fair scheduling environment it is not easy for an application to decide if a certain number of threads might cause an oversubscription of the computational resources. However, given a static scheduling strategy on the application level, overloading can be identified as an artifact in the graph of the average execution time of the parallel code section.

To show this effect, we can use the same test scenario as described in Sect. 2 simply by changing the parallelization of application A from Intel TBB to OpenMP using a static scheduling policy (the default scheduling strategy of OpenMP). The solid line in Fig. 3 shows the average execution time of such modified application A on an approximately idle system, depending on the number of threads $x \in \{1, ..., 4N\}$. In a second experiment A was executed concurrently to application B, which also was performing heavy calculations utilizing a fixed number of $r = 4$ threads. The result of this experiment is visualized in the dashed line of Fig. 3.

Interestingly both graphs show an artifact, one at $x = 9$ and the other at $x = 5$. As we know that the machine has a total of eight cores the artifacts are clearly a sign of oversubscription as they appear exactly when the total number of busy threads $x + r$ exceeds the number of available cores N. We were able to reproduce this effect not only on the Windows 7 machine but also on machines with OpenSUSE Linux and SUSE Linux Enterprise Server.

In the remainder of this section we will develop a simple model in order to explain this artifact as a result of the scheduling strategy of the operating system and the static scheduling of OpenMP. Based on the model we think that this specific scheduling configuration will reliably produce such artifact when testing various numbers of threads for a parallel code section. As a result this artifact can be exploited as a detector for system wide oversubscription on the application level.

Given a multicore system with N cores ($N \in \mathbb{N}$, $N > 0$) and assuming that a number of r threads are already running within the system environment, we will estimate the amount of computational resources an application gets granted when utilizing x threads ($x, r \in \mathbb{N}$, $x, r \geq 0$). In order to simplify things we require all threads to be always ready to run (as it is the case if only computational resources are consumed within the parallel section). Furthermore, we require the thread scheduling to be based on the following three scheduling heuristics:

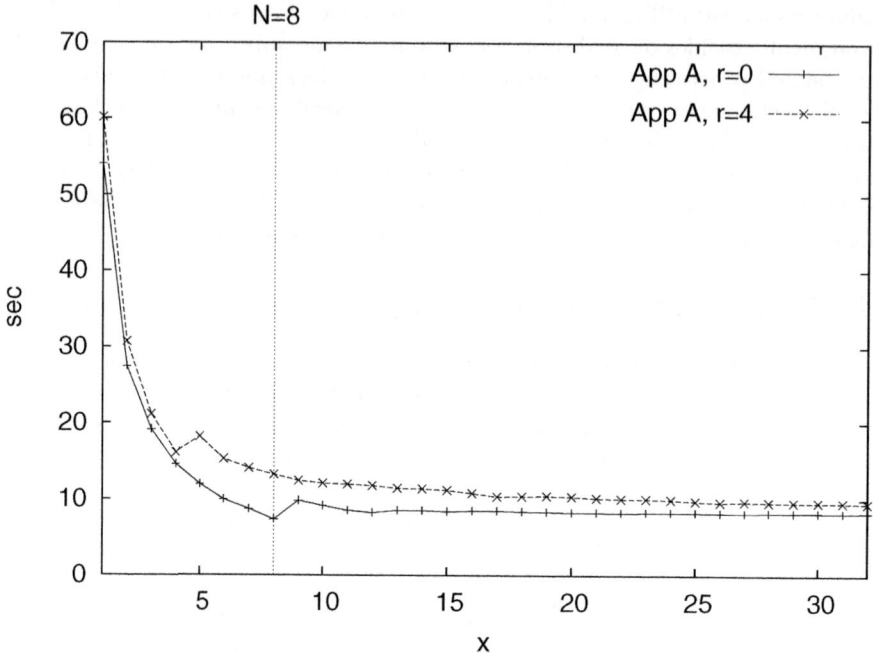

Fig. 3. Visualization of the average execution time of application A. The red line shows the performance on an approximately idle system. The green line shows the results for application A being executed concurrently to another application, which is utilizing $r = 4$ threads for its calculations.

- Fair Scheduling: The scheduler deals out time slices to all threads in the system in a uniform way (as long as they have the same priority, which we assume here).
- Load Balancing: The scheduler tries to spread all threads of a process equally across all available cores. Threads of different processes are dealt to the cores in a way that balances the load among all cores.
- Pinning to PEs: The scheduler tries to run each thread always on the same PE in order to optimize cache reuse.

A scheduler following these three heuristics is the Windows thread scheduler [4], but other operating systems are using these heuristics as well.

As a result of these heuristics all $r + x$ threads are distributed equally over all available PEs and due to the pinning of the threads to PEs this assignment is relatively stable. Knowing this we can compute the minimum number of threads running by turns on each of the N PEs:

$$\delta_{min} := max\left(\left\lfloor \frac{r + x}{N} \right\rfloor, 1\right) \ . \tag{2}$$

Note that in the trivial case, where fewer threads occupy the system than PEs available, each thread is executed in parallel on one PE. We set $\delta_{min} := 1$ for this special case.

As the r threads were distributed prior to the x threads we know that at least one of the x threads is sharing its PE with δ_{max} others:

$$\delta_{max} := \left\lceil \frac{r+x}{N} \right\rceil .$$

(3)

In our model the r threads are assumed to run forever, but computing resources may become available when some of the x threads terminate while others are still running. So in reality the actual contention factor δ lays somewhere in between the upper and lower bound:

$$\delta_{min} \le \delta \le \delta_{max} .$$

(4)

This contention factor δ can then be used to estimate the amount of parallel computing resources which will be granted to an application allocating x individual threads:

$$n(x, \delta) := min\left(\frac{x}{\delta}, N\right) .$$

(5)

The restriction of $n(x, \delta)$ is justified by the fact that we only have a maximum of N cores available - so a value larger than that would not make sense.

Using the parallel computing resources from (5) we can estimate the average execution time for a parallel code section as follows:

$$t(x, \delta) := \mathcal{L}\left(\frac{1}{n(x, \delta)}\right) ,$$

(6)

with $\mathcal{L} : \mathbb{R} \to \mathbb{R}$ being a linear transformation, taking into account a scaling by a constant factor (depending on the work done in the parallel section) and also the addition of a constant term not depending on x (for example sequential parts of the code).

The solid line in Fig. 4 shows the measurements of the previous experiment where the oversubscription of computational resources occurs at $x > 4$. In addition to that, the minimum and maximum bounds $t(x, \delta_{min})$ and $t(x, \delta_{max})$ for the average execution time are visualized. Note that the bounds in this figure have been transformed linearly to fit the data points.

The reason why the experimental measurements show only one peak, despite the function $t(x, \delta_{max})$ predicting a peak every N steps, is that with growing x the work distributed on the individual threads will be of a finer granularity. Due to that the scheduler can reschedule threads between cores with lower contention more often, evening out the artifacts. This is covered by the model, as it predicts the contention factor δ to lie between δ_{min} and δ_{max}.

A static scheduling policy is required in order to see the artifact in the first place. If remaining tasks can be processed by idle threads (as it is the case for

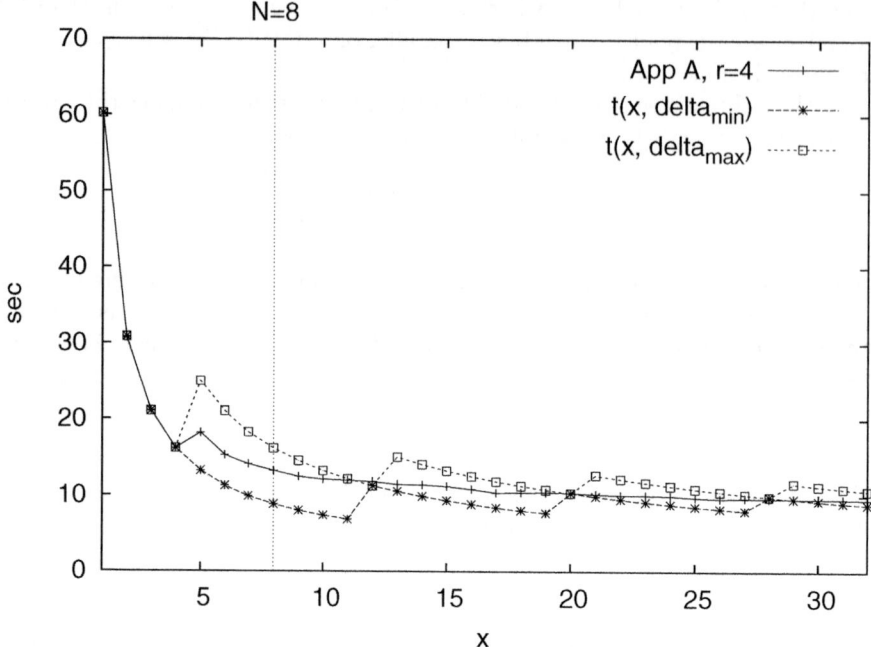

Fig. 4. Fitting of the upper and lower bounds to the experimental data

OpenMP's dynamic scheduling) the artifacts are evened out. This rescheduling of tasks on a fine granular level is the reason why the artifact also does not show up in average execution time of an application being parallelized using Intel TBB (as visualized in Fig. 1).

Based on the proposed analysis we have strong evidence that artifacts in the expected execution time which result from varying the thread count of a parallel section are a sign for oversubscription - as long as the scheduling heuristics mentioned above are used by the operating system and as long as a static scheduling is used for the parallelization.

Note that this artifacts can be observed clearly in the range $x \in [1, N]$, which is the range we are actually interested in when trying to prevent system wide overloading of computational resources. Using this simple model an oversubscription detection can be build into an application which then prevents oversubscription of the computational resources on the application level. More or less this leads to a defensive steering, which helps the application to just use unused computational resources. However, in practice a varying load on the system could even out the artifact, which makes the oversubscription hard to detect - but such intermittent oversubscription is also less painful for other applications. Due to the fact that the average execution time requires multiple runs for a different number of threads this method is rather applicable to a calibration phase at the beginning instead of a constant optimization done at runtime.

5   Related Work

Much research has been done, typically in the field of auto-tuning, adapting various program parameters in order to achieve a better parallel performance (examples are [5], [6], [7]). The number of processors or threads used in a parallel code section is often one important parameter, but generally the research focuses on maximizing the throughput of one application and does not examine the behavior of multiple applications in the same system environment.

Taking into account multiple programs in a shared system environment, a technique is presented in [8] to achieve better cost-efficiency on shared memory machines by varying the number of used processors in a parallel section. Related to that, in [9] an approach is presented that adaptively manages a pool of threads for multiple programs; it gradually de-allocates threads from programs making ineffective use of parallelism and allocates them to programs making effective use of parallelism based on run-time performance measurements.

In [10] the authors discuss the benefits of extending operating systems with auto-tuning capabilities. They argue that incorporating an auto-tuning mechanism as a component of the operating system will allow a global optimization taking into account the whole system environment.

Another solution that tackles the oversubscription problem on the operating system level is to perform a multi-level scheduling instead of treating all threads the same. Doing this each application running in the system gets a well defined percentage of processing time, which can then be distributed among all threads belonging to a given process. The consequence is that an application can no longer negatively affect other applications when utilizing too many threads. Multi-level scheduling based on groups has been available in the Linux kernel since version 2.6.24. Administrators can configure the system so that new processes are put in groups based on certain characteristics, e.g. the user that started the process. The groups are then given a fair share of the resources. However, this system was difficult to set up. In November 2010 a kernel patch introduced automatic grouping of processes based on terminal sessions, which provides a good default solution for desktop systems [11].

The impact of MPI, OpenMP and UPC implementations of the NAS Parallel Benchmarks on various multisocket architectures is evaluated in [12]. In this work the authors oversubscribed a dedicated environment and also tested the throughput if multiple benchmarks were running in a shared or partitioned environment. The results indicate that in specific situations the oversubscription of cores by applications within a competitive environment can have positive effects for application and system throughput. This stands in contrast to the findings of our experiment in Sect. 2. However, the positive effects in [12] did only occur if the workloads had different resource consumption characteristics (compute vs. memory intensive). If workloads were the same, as they are in our experiment, also [12]observed negative effects for the applications.

6   Conclusion

In this paper we demonstrated the impact of oversubscription of computational resources in the context of a simple desktop scenario. We showed that using too many threads in one application can lead to performance loss for other applications in the same system environment. We also showed how common parallelization tools are trying to exploit the available computational resources while not causing oversubscription. As a result of this analysis we have the finding that none of the examined tools offers a mechanism to effectively take into account the load of the system. Furthermore, we presented an approach to detect oversubscription as an artifact in the average execution time of a parallel code section.

It is important to point out that oversubscription is not always a bad thing. It should be avoided if the limiting factor of the application are the computational resources. However, oversubscription can have positive effects as well if other resources are relevant for the application's execution [13] or if the characteristics of resource consumption of competing applications in the desktop scenario are not the same [12].

A number of questions are raised by this study. One is how other parallelization tools, which we did not examine for this study, achieve an optimal exploitation of resources on the one hand, while preventing oversubscription on the other hand? What consequences do the various scheduling policies of today's operating systems have regarding the effects of oversubscription? And the most important question is: How can negative effects of oversubscription be prevented effectively and at which level should this mechanism be implemented? Our results suggest that it is not easy to do on an application level alone, but under special conditions it can be possible.

References

1. Intel: Intel threading building blocks. Intel Tutorial (2007)
2. Board, O.A.R.: Openmp application program interface (2008)
3. Fuentes, E.: Throttling concurrency in the clr 4.0 threadpool. MSDN Magazine (2010)
4. Russinovich, M.E., Solomon, D., Ionescu, A.: Windows Internals: Book and Online Course Bundle. C.B.Learning, United Kingdom (2010)
5. Tabatabaee, V., Tiwari, A., Hollingsworth, J.K.: Parallel parameter tuning for applications with performance variability. In: Proceedings of the 2005 ACM/IEEE Conference on Supercomputing, SC 2005, p. 57. IEEE Computer Society, Washington, DC (2005)
6. Qasem, A., Kennedy, K., Mellor-Crummey, J.: Automatic tuning of whole applications using direct search and a performance-based transformation system, vol. 36, pp. 183–196. Kluwer Academic Publishers, Hingham (2006)
7. Ganapathi, A., Datta, K., Fox, A., Patterson, D.: A case for machine learning to optimize multicore performance. In: Proceedings of the First USENIX Conference on Hot Topics in Parallelism, HotPar 2009, p. 1. USENIX Association, Berkeley, CA (2009)

8. Reimer, N.: Dynamically Adapting the Degree of Parallelism With Reflexive Programs. In: Saad, Y., Yang, T., Ferreira, A., Rolim, J.D.P. (eds.) IRREGULAR 1996. LNCS, vol. 1117, pp. 313–318. Springer, Heidelberg (1996)

9. Hall, M.W., Martonosi, M.: Adaptive parallelism in compiler-parallelized code. In: Proc. of the 2nd SUIF Compiler Workshop (1997)

10. Karcher, T., Schaefer, C., Pankratius, V.: Auto-tuning support for manycore applications: perspectives for operating systems and compilers. SIGOPS Oper. Syst. Rev. 43(2), 96–97 (2009)

11. Corbet, J.: TTY-based group scheduling (November 2010), http://lwn.net/Articles/415740/ (retrieved on: January 13, 2011)

12. Iancu, C., Hofmeyr, S., Blagojevic, F., Zheng, Y.: Oversubscription on multicore processors. In: 2010 IEEE International Symposium on Parallel Distributed Processing (IPDPS), pp. 1–11 (2010)

13. Mattson, T., Sanders, B., Massingill, B.: Patterns for parallel programming, 1st edn. Addison-Wesley Professional (2004)

Capturing Transactional Memory Application's Behavior – The Prerequisite for Performance Analysis

Martin Schindewolf and Wolfgang Karl

Chair for Computer Architecture and Parallel Processing,
Karlsruhe Institute of Technology (KIT),
Kaiserstr. 128,
76131 Karlsruhe, Germany
{schindewolf,karl}@kit.edu

Abstract. Programmers need tool support to detect and localize performance bottlenecks in Transactional Memory applications. To employ these tools, the genuine TM application's behavior must be preserved. Consequently, this paper presents a methodology and an implementation to capture event logs *representing the behavior* of a transactional memory application. We compare our approach with a state-of-the-art binary translation tool (Pin) and study the impact of the trace generation on the throughput of the STM system and the conflicts detected between transactions. Additionally we evaluate a multi-threaded event trace compression scheme that reduces the size of the trace files and decreases the write bandwidth demands.

1 Introduction

Herlihy and Moss proposed Transactional Memory (TM) with the intention to simplify synchronization in multi-threaded shared memory programs [9]. In contrast to previous synchronization approaches, Transactional Memory features the optimistic execution of critical sections. Conflicts between transactions are tracked by a runtime system that is implemented in hardware or software. Software implementations are user-level libraries, called Software Transactional Memory (STM), that run on commodity hardware. Recent research addresses the detection of bottlenecks and the visualization of TM applications [18]. However, one aspect is not covered sufficiently: how can the programmer capture the genuine TM application's behavior? This is an important prerequisite for the performance analysis and the detection of bottlenecks. Although frameworks to profile TM applications have already been proposed [1,16,11,5], none of these approaches accomplishes to capture *all* transactionally relevant events while at the same time having modest write bandwidth demands. This paper contributes to the state-of-the-art by employing online compression algorithms in order to reduce the amount of data to be written to hard disk. We demonstrate for the STAMP benchmark suite that the influence on the runtimes is reduced significantly compared to buffered tracing, and compression can reduce the data

V. Pankratius and M. Philippsen (Eds.): MSEPT 2012, LNCS 7303, pp. 30–41, 2012.

volume by a factor of 10.8. We study the side effects of trace generation on the application in detail. By studying an application with high write demands, the advantages of online compressing trace data become obvious. In case the application thread also compresses the buffer, the application behavior is changed since this time is not spent on regular execution. Thus, conflicts will not manifest and the behavior is changed. Thus, we introduce dedicated compression threads that are assigned to one application thread. The application thread only fills the buffer and hands it to the compression thread. Of course this comes at the cost of increased computational demands. We implement the trace compression on top of a lightweight trace generation scheme that has a low influence on the application. With this scheme, the application generates an authentic trace file that preserves the original course of events for advanced post-processing steps (e.g., performance analysis and visualization).

2 Related Work

Event traces are usually obtained through running an instrumented application. Dynamic approaches often use dynamic binary instrumentation to instrument a running application. E.g., Pin is a dynamic compilation tool that features portable, transparent, and efficient instrumentation [12]. DynamoRIO belongs to the same category but differs in implementation details [3]. Valgrind is specialized on memory instructions and more heavy-weight [13]. Static instrumentation approaches often use libraries to log events. The Open Trace Format employs ASCII events and focuses on scalability and read performance [10]. More formats are the Pablo Self-defining trace format and Pajé [2,14]. Epilog is a representative for a binary trace format [17] and Intel's structured trace format (STF) for a proprietary trace format[1].

Herlihy and Moss proposed Transactional Memory (TM) with the intention to simplify synchronization in multi-threaded shared memory programs [9]. With TM, a programmer groups lines of code to a transaction. Transactions execute with special properties: atomicity, consistency and isolation [8]. Software Transactional Memory systems rely on software primitives to ensure these transactional properties [15]. In this paper, we augment an STM library, called TinySTM [6], with low-overhead event logging facilities. Recently, the visualization and optimization of TM application's behavior in a C# environment has been achieved [18]. This work is an excellent example for the many possibilities to exploit runtime information in a post processing step. This approach executes tracing tasks in parallel with the garbage collector to minimize the application disturbance. The garbage collector is characteristic for a *managed language*. In case of an *unmanaged language*, such as C or C++, different solutions are needed. For our approach (application and STM written in C), we present a more general solution in this paper. In the context of an object-based STM, profiling and in particular metrics to rate the application have been explored [1]. A Haskell-specific profiling framework has been proposed in [16]. Discrete event simulation has been

---

[1] Intel[®] Corp., Intel[R] Cluster Tools.

shown to support the development of TM contention managers [5]. Further, a low-overhead monitoring framework has been proposed [11]. None of these approaches has explored techniques for compression nor did these works compare their performance with a binary-instrumentation tool.

3   TM-Specific Trace Generation

Event traces record the timely occurrence of events initiated through the application. Information retrieved from these event traces is often used to improve the application's runtime behavior (e.g., find memory access patterns with higher spatial and temporal locality). One key point is that obtaining these event traces does not change the application behavior, which is called non-intrusive tracing. In some experimental setups, the goal of non-intrusiveness can be achieved with smaller costs than in others. Unfortunately, a perfect solution for generating traces does not exist. In this paper we research and evaluate how to ameliorate the costs of logging events.

3.1   Minimizing Application Disturbances

The trace generation introduces overhead when logging events during the runtime of the application. This overhead may influence two important performance metrics of a TM application: throughput and number of aborted transactions. The non-uniform delay of threads when logging events may influence both metrics. Delayed threads may lead to additionally detected conflicts. With TM this effect is more severe than with mutual exclusive synchronization: A conflict leads to a rollback of one transaction and all previous modifications of the transactions are undone and recomputed. In case this conflict is artificially generated through delaying the thread by the tracing machinery, the recorded application behavior is not genuine. Hence, avoiding additional delays is one goal. Threads may be delayed when writing the logged events from a buffer to the hard disk. In prior work Knüpfer et al. propose to store a trace of n threads [processes] with $1...n$ streams [10]. If the number of streams is less than n, additional synchronization is introduced to coordinate two threads that write to the same stream. In our use case this synchronization comes with the undesired side-effect of artificially delaying threads. Therefore, we only allow a bijective mapping of n threads to n streams – e.g., each thread writes to a separate file. In contrast to previous approaches [10], the trace generation is not encapsulated inside a dedicated library due to performance reasons. The STM library already stores meta data in thread local storage. Through extending the meta data and manually inserting calls to log events, we achieve a higher data locality. Further, the compiler may inline and optimize the tracing code and achieve a higher performance compared with call back-based approaches. The interface of the TinySTM remains unchanged, thus, this tracing approach is also transparent to the application developer. The event logging mechanisms are integrated in the build process of the STM in a way that these are easily accessible for users.

The design choices follow the need to preserve the original course of events. In order to reduce the interference between threads, each thread writes to a separate trace file. The corresponding file handles are stored in the thread local storage. Also, functions to read the OS time and cycle counter (TSC) were added. Event traces may be captured in two different formats: as ASCII or as binary packets. The format of the binary packets is shown in Table 1. The transactional events are captured by instrumenting the respective STM functions. We took care when placing the instrumentation such that events will not be logged prematurely: e.g., after entering the function stm_commit, the transaction may still

Table 1. Format of timing and transactional events in x86_64 binary trace files

Type 8 Bit	Payload 64 Bit	Payload2 64 Bit
Timing1	tx [%p]	OS time [sec]
Timing2	OS time [nsec]	padding
RTSC	TSC [cycles]	padding
Start	tx [%p]	STM counter
Read[1]	address	padding
Write[1]	address	value
Commit	tx [%p]	STM counter
Abort	tx [%p]	STM counter

abort during the validation of the read and write sets. The ASCII mode introduces one fprintf call per event. This first approach writes elements of varying size at once whereas the binary tracing approach buffers events of fixed size in a dedicated local memory buffer. The buffer size is given in number of event elements. A $10K$ element buffer signifies that each thread allocates a buffer of $136[bit] * 10K \approx 166KBytes$.

3.2   Implication of Lightweight Trace Generation on Offline Analysis

The goal of a lightweight tracing scheme is to reduce the runtime disturbances of the application. A trade-off between logging heavy-weight events with high precision and lightweight events with low precision must be found. Then, an advanced offline analysis can reconstruct the original course of events. Having a precise notion of time is mandatory for visualization and especially for finding causalities among the traced events. In the following, we propose to reconstruct the time line of events based on the very scarce usage of a heavy-weight time stamp and the frequent logging of a lightweight cycle counter. In contrast to vector clocks [7], that capture the causality of events and preserve a partial ordering, our approach interpolates the real time when an event occurred. The function clock_gettime delivers the time synchronized across all processing cores (heavy-weight). At Start, Abort, and Commit events, the cycle counter of the core is logged (with the RDTSC[2] instruction). Despite being lightweight, this counter comes with the disadvantage of not being synchronized across cores. Through also logging it at thread init and exit, both time stamps are correlated. During offline processing, the time between two events (e.g. thread init and start) is calculated according to $\Delta t = \frac{\Delta c}{f}$ where f is the frequency of the core and Δc is the number of cycles between the two events. By adding Δt to the heavy-weight synchronized time stamp (at initialization of the thread), the real time of each event is reconstructed. Transactional events in between start and commit are

---

[2] RDTSC is not influenced by dynamic voltage and frequency scaling of the cores.

interpolated by assuming that each event consumes an equal amount of time. Further, repeating these steps for all threads, enables to establish an order of the concurrently generated events.

3.3　The Influence of Tracing on the Runtime

In the following, we will use a TM application, called *bank*, to study the influence of the tracing machinery on the runtime of the application. *bank* manages a fixed number of bank accounts and transfers money between them with transactions. Long running read-only transactions are carried out in turn with short writing transactions. Since *bank* spends most time in-

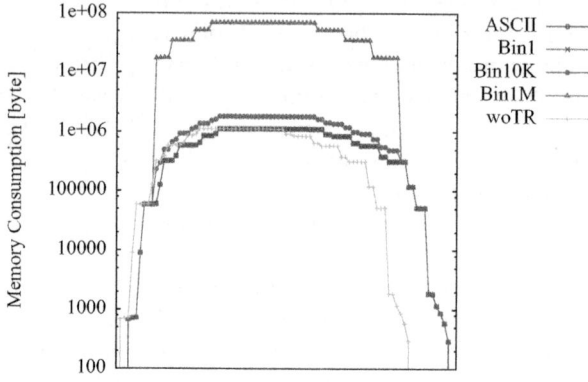

Fig. 1. Heap size of bank application

side transactions, it is a useful stress test for the tracing machinery because of the high write bandwidth demands. Hence, *bank* is chosen to study the influence of the trace generation on the memory consumption and TM metrics.

Memory consumption at runtime is illustrated in Figure 1. More precisely the graphs represent the heap size of the running application with different tracing variants. These results are generated with `valgrind` [13] in particular employing the tool `massif` to sample the memory consumption. The x-axis shows the sampling points in time where the heap size is determined. The memory consumption without tracing (woTR), ASCII tracing (ASCII), and binary tracing with different buffer sizes: 1 element (Bin1), $10K$ elements (Bin10K) and $1M$ elements (Bin1M) are shown on the y-axis in a logarithmic scale. Bin1M dominates all variants with 70 MBytes memory consumption at most. The average heap consumption for the pure application `bank` is less than 1.2 MBytes. Increasing the buffer size to $10K$ elements increases memory requirements to 1.8 MBytes. The memory demands are negligible compared to the available memory in most desktop machines (around 4 GBytes). The increased memory requirements lead to a larger cache footprint which may have a severe impact on the application as it may lead to more cache misses. To demonstrate the adequateness of the increased memory requirements, we compare our customized trace generation with a state-of-the-art dynamic instrumentation tool called Pin [12]. Instrumentation is achieved through so called Pintools which are written in `C/C++`. At runtime Pin uses binary instrumentation to connect the unmodified application and the Pintool. A Pintool usually consists of two parts: an instrumentation and an analysis part. In our case, the instrumentation registers call backs for the

STM functions[3] start, commit, abort and thread create and exit. The analysis part logs the events and writes them to a file. However, not all events are available with the Pintool - only the ones underlined in Table 1 are logged. At thread create and exit the trace files are opened and closed respectively. In order to enable a fair comparison to our approach each thread writes to a separate file directly and, hence is comparable with ASCII or Bin1.

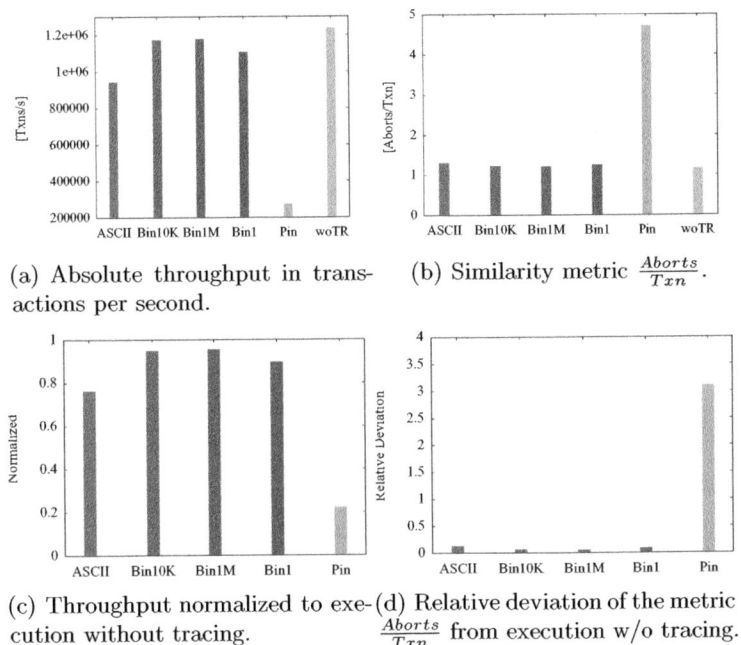

(a) Absolute throughput in transactions per second.

(b) Similarity metric $\frac{Aborts}{Txn}$.

(c) Throughput normalized to execution without tracing.

(d) Relative deviation of the metric $\frac{Aborts}{Txn}$ from execution w/o tracing.

Fig. 2. Influence of trace generation on the TM behavior

Influence on the application's behavior as mentioned before, shared memory applications, featuring separate threads of execution are sensitive to modifications. Because these modifications are necessary to generate event traces, the overhead of generating event traces and the influence of the experimental setup on the application's runtime behavior must be studied. As a first indicator which combination of tracing and experimental setup is suited, we investigate the influence on the throughput of the application. The application *bank* runs for a fixed period of time (by default 10 seconds). During this time, the amount of transactions executed per second is measured. Figure 2(a) depicts this throughput. Correspondingly, Figure 2(c) holds the normalized throughput, which is computed according to $\frac{Txns_X}{Txns_{woTR}}$, where X selects the tracing variant and *woTR* means execution without tracing. These performance numbers show that the Pintool limits the throughput in transactions per second to 22 % whereas all proposed variants reach more than 76 %.

---

[3] For full traces transactional loads and stores are also instrumented.

Further, we seek to quantify the influence of tracing on the TM characteristics. Due to the optimistic nature of transactional execution, transactions may conflict with each other. Resolving these conflicts usually leads to an abort of one of the transactions. When combining the rate of aborts with the rate of transactions, a metric is found that serves as a measure for similarity of transactional execution (computed as $\frac{Aborts}{Txn}$). In case the application is not affected by the tracing machinery, the metric yields similar values because the amount of aborts experienced per transaction is similar. Figure 2(b) shows this similarity metric for our tracing variants and Pin. Computed according to the formula $(X - woTR)/woTR$, Figure 2(d) demonstrates the relative deviation of the tracing variants compared without tracing. Since a smaller deviation means similar program behavior, our tracing variants preserve the application's behavior better than Pin.

3.4   Online Trace Compression

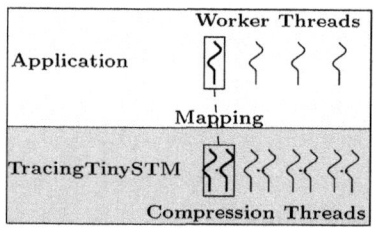

Fig. 3. TracingTinySTM with support for online trace compression

In a multi-core system with a large number of threads executing and generating traces concurrently, the write bandwidth of the hard disk soon becomes the bottleneck. Therefore, compressing the trace data prior to writing it to disk seems a viable solution. However, compression algorithms have to be carried out by or on behalf of the application thread. This poses a major challenge if the application is not to be influenced by the compression. As one of our declared goals is to minimize the disturbance of the application, having the application thread compress the data is counterproductive. While carrying out the compression the thread would execute non-transactional code instead of playing its original role with the other threads. Therefore our approach decouples trace generation (done by the application or worker threads) and trace compression (carried out by compression threads). This basic principle is also illustrated in Figure 3. Due to the API of the TinySTM, compression threads are spawned and destroyed transparently to the user. E.g., when a thread initializes its transactional state, a predefined number of compression threads is created. These threads will then compress a buffer of fixed size when signaled by the application thread. However, writing or compressing a buffer takes different amounts of time. Thus, a suitable mapping of application to compression threads must be found. In [10] the use of the ZLIB library[4] for compression has been proposed. Our first experiments revealed that a thread mapping of roughly 1:10 would be necessary to keep the application thread from waiting. Thus, our approach uses the slightly different Lempel-Ziv-Oberhumer (LZO) library which is designed for real-time compression[5]. Although the additional speed comes at the cost of a lower compression

---

[4] J. Gailly and M. Adler, zlib, http://www.zlib.net/

[5] M. F. Xaver and J. Oberhumer, LZO, http://www.oberhumer.com/opensource/lzo/

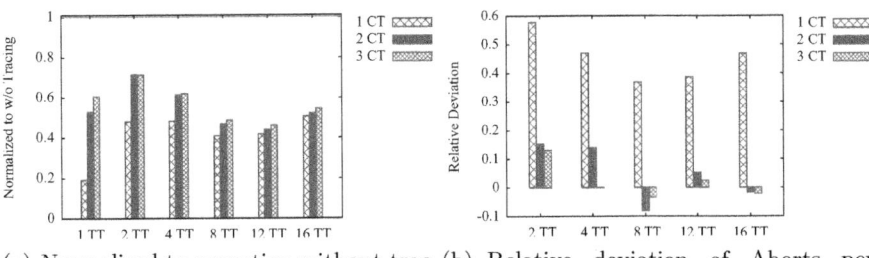

(a) Normalized to execution without tracing.

(b) Relative deviation of Aborts per
Transaction compared without tracing.

Fig. 4. Throughput and similarity with multi-threaded trace compression

rate, the results are still satisfying. The LZO library compresses $4,607$ MBytes
to 156 MBytes yielding a compression factor of 29. However, this is also due to
the fact that the binary format contains padding which compresses easily.

The throughput of the application threads executing without tracing is compared
with different mappings of application to compression threads for trace compression. E.g., 2CT signifies that 1 application thread maps to 2 dedicated compression threads. These compression threads compress data inside a buffer by calling
the LZO library. 1CT and 3CT are constructed accordingly. Figure 4(a) shows
the Txn/s normalized to execution without tracing. This throughput ranges
between 44% and 71%. This is a serious drop when compared to tracing without
compression which can be
ascribed to the larger memory
footprint. More buffers need to
be utilized by the tracing thread
and executing the LZO routines
also has an impact on the instruction cache. Further, more threads
share the same computational
resources which are eventually
saturated. We argue that the similarity in the application behavior is more important than the
measured throughput. Figure 4(b)
shows that all tracing variants ex-

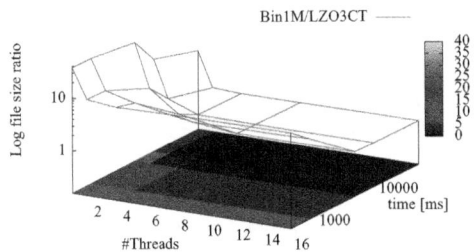

Fig. 5. Compression factor computed as
$\frac{Size_{Bin1M}}{Size_{LZO3CT}}$ as a function of thread count and
computation time (with logarithmic z scale)

cept 1CT capture the application behavior in an acceptable way because the
relative deviations of the $\frac{Aborts}{Txn}$ are smaller than 15%. A negative deviation
means that execution without tracing has a lower $\frac{Aborts}{Txn}$ rate. Therefore, the
setups with LZO2CT and LZO3CT are adequate for trace generation.

The compression factor of the LZO3CT scheme compared with the Bin1M setup
is shown in Figure 5. LZO3CT efficiently reduces the size of the log files when

the thread count is low. Further, the runtime of the *bank* application should not exceed 5 s to benefit from reduced file sizes. This time span is comparable with simulators for TM that run for one day.

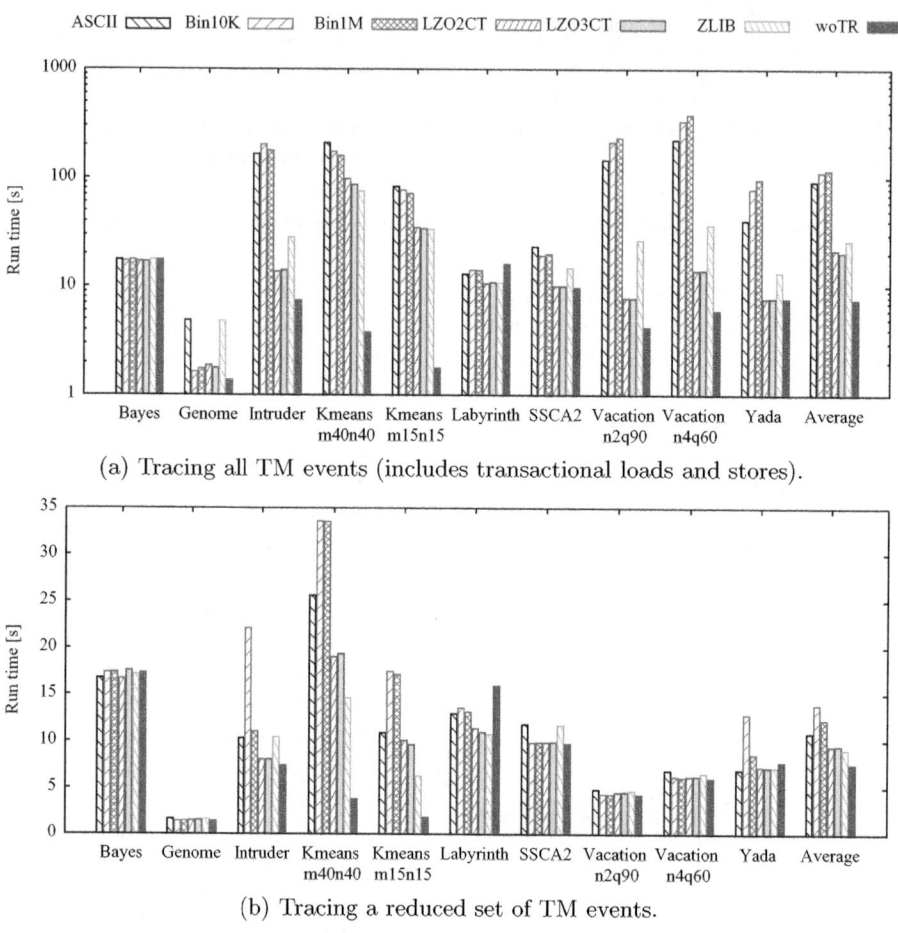

(a) Tracing all TM events (includes transactional loads and stores).

(b) Tracing a reduced set of TM events.

Fig. 6. Average execution times of the STAMP benchmarks

4   Impact of Trace Generation on STAMP Benchmarks

In this section, we study the impact of the proposed trace generation schemes on the execution of TM benchmarks that stem from multiple application domains. The architecture used in our experiments comprises two Intel Xeon CPUs (called Westmere) each with 6 cores and hyper-threading technology. Westmere implements the Nehalem microarchitecture and is implemented in

32 nm technology. It features 24 hardware threads in total. Each core has an exclusive L1 and L2 cache (cf. Table 2). L3 caches are shared inside a socket. For our experiments all benchmarks from the STAMP TM suite [4] run consecutively and to completion. The tracing functionality is implemented inside the TinySTM (version 0.9.9) [6]. Each of the 10 STAMP

Table 2. Experimental platform

Intel(R) Xeon(R) CPU	X5670 @ 2.93GHz
CPU frequency	1596 MHz
Processing Units per Core	2
L1 size	32KB each
L2 size	256KB each
L3 size	12MB each
Number of Cores	12 total
Number of Hardware Threads	24 total
Number of Sockets	2

benchmarks solves a problem of fixed size. All reported values are averages over 30 runs to compensate for variations in the execution. Each benchmark runs with 8 worker threads. The thread count is sufficient because the STAMP applications show a limited scalability on this architecture. The trace scenarios are as follows: **ASCII**: traces generated are in the ASCII format without buffering, **Bin***: binary traces with a 10K and 1M element buffer, **LZOkCT**: LZO compression with k compression threads for each worker thread, **ZLIB**: ZLIB compression without compression threads, **woTR**: without any tracing enabled. Figures 6(a)

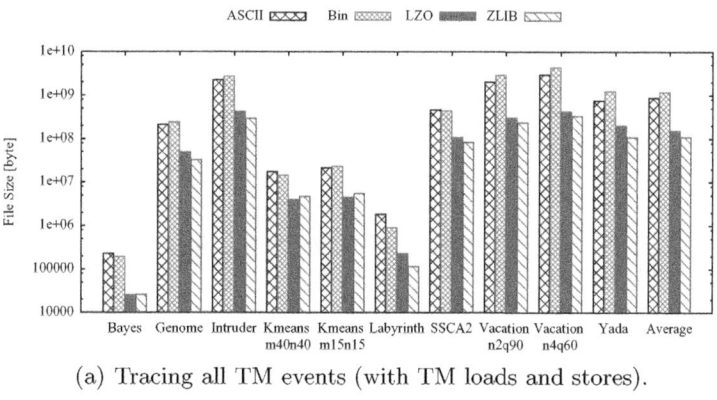

(a) Tracing all TM events (with TM loads and stores).

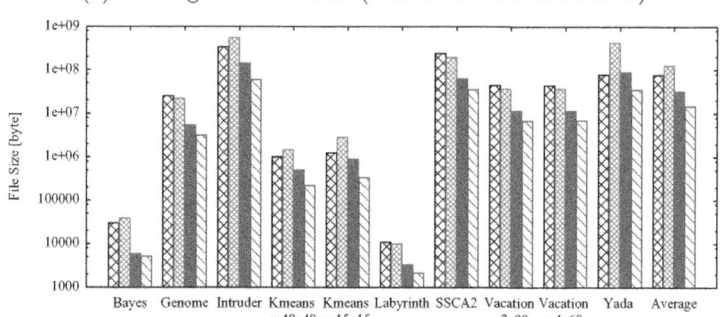

(b) Tracing a reduced set of TM events.

Fig. 7. File sizes for traces of the STAMP benchmarks

and 6(b) depict the execution times of each individual STAMP benchmark with and without tracing and the computed average over all benchmarks. The average shows the largest increase in runtime for the ASCII and plain binary tracing variants. The *Labyrinth* application surprisingly shows a speed up when tracing is enabled.

We investigated this case and found that the runtime of *Labyrinth* has a high variance. Further measurements revealed that the number of L3 misses is lower for the tracing variants. The adjacent Table 3 holds the range and average value of these misses.

This is an unusual case that eventually leads to a small speedup. The

Table 3. L3 cache misses for *Labyrinth*

Setup	L3 cache misses		
	Min	Max	Average
woTR	$1.7\,10^7$	$2.1\,10^8$	$9.9\,10^7$
Bin1M	$1.1\,10^7$	$1.6\,10^8$	$4.8\,10^7$
LZO2CT	$1.2\,10^7$	$1.2\,10^8$	$2.8\,10^7$

common case is e.g., *Kmeans* that shows that the tracing threads are competing with the application threads for architectural resources. This competition leads to additional stall cycles and increases the cache miss rate; eventually contributing to an increased execution time. Execution times increase substantially, when *all* transactional events are traced (cf. to Figure 6(a)). Please note the logarithmic y scale, which also emphasizes the prolonged times of ASCII and Bin*. Herewith, the benefits of the online compression approaches are demonstrated. On average LZO3CT yields a 30 % better runtime than ZLIB and 451 % better than Bin10K. The runtime effects are not as prominent in Figure 6(b), when tracing only a *subset* of the TM events. Figure 7(a) and 7(b) shows the average sizes of the trace files with and without compression. Again, please note the logarithmic y-axis. Regardless of the amount of data, the ZLIB library provides a higher compression ratio on average. For the small event set, the LZO library only yields a compression factor of 3.94 compared with 8.63 for ZLIB. For the large event set, LZO compresses with a factor of 7.82 and ZLIB with a factor equal to 10.79 on average.

5   Conclusion

In this paper, we propose a TM-specific solution for capturing and preserving the TM application's behavior. TM events are logged, buffered and compressed inside a word-based Software Transactional Memory library. This approach substantially increases the throughput and reduces the application disturbance in comparison with a state-of-the-art binary translation tool (Pin). The more sophisticated trace generation variants employ compression algorithms to reduce the amount of data to be written. The ZLIB and the LZO compression schemes are compared with the non-compressing variants. The results show that especially adding dedicated compression threads does have benefits: for large data sets the influence on the runtime is reduced significantly. The trace data is compressed with a factor of up to 10. The compression ratio of the ZLIB algorithm is superior to LZO, but also leads to an increased runtime for large data sets.

Future work could transfer the presented techniques to larger and non-symmetric systems (e.g., DSM systems). Then, the scalability of the presented techniques should be evaluated.

References

1. Ansari, M., Jarvis, K., Kotselidis, C., Lujan, M., Kirkham, C., Watson, I.: Profiling Transactional Memory Applications. In: Proceedings of the 17th Euromicro Conference, pp. 11–20 (2009)
2. Aydt, R.A.: The pablo self-defining data format. Tech. rep., Urbana, Illinois 61801, USA (1994), http://wotug.org/parallel/performance/tools/pablo/
3. Bruening, D., Garnett, T., Amarasinghe, S.: An infrastructure for adaptive dynamic optimization. In: CGO 2003, pp. 265–275 (2003)
4. Cao Minh, C., Chung, J., Kozyrakis, C., Olukotun, K.: STAMP: Stanford transactional applications for multi-processing. In: IISWC 2008 (September 2008)
5. Demsky, B., Dash, A.: Using discrete event simulation to analyze contention managers. International Journal of Parallel Programming, 1–26 (2011)
6. Felber, P., Fetzer, C., Riegel, T.: Dynamic performance tuning of word-based software transactional memory. In: Proceedings of the 13th PPoPP 2008, pp. 237–246 (2008)
7. Fidge, C.J.: Timestamps in message-passing systems that preserve the partial ordering. In: Proceedings of the 11th ACSC, vol. 10(1), pp. 56–66 (1988)
8. Harris, T., Larus, J., Rajwar, R.: Transactional Memory, 2nd edn., vol. 5. Morgan & Claypool Publishers (2010); Synthesis Lectures on Computer Architecture
9. Herlihy, M., Moss, J.E.B.: Transactional Memory: Architectural Support For Lock-free Data Structures. In: Proceedings of the 20th Annual International Symposium on Computer Architecture, pp. 289–300. IEEE (May 1993)
10. Knüpfer, A., Brendel, R., Brunst, H., Mix, H., Nagel, W.: Introducing the Open Trace Format (OTF). In: Alexandrov, V.N., van Albada, G.D., Sloot, P.M.A., Dongarra, J. (eds.) ICCS 2006. LNCS, vol. 3992, pp. 526–533. Springer, Heidelberg (2006)
11. Lourenço, J., Dias, R., Luís, J., Rebelo, M., Pessanha, V.: Understanding the behavior of transactional memory applications. In: Proceedings of the 7th PADTAD Workshop 2009, pp. 3:1–3:9. ACM, New York (2009)
12. Luk, C.K., Cohn, R., Muth, R., Patil, H., Klauser, A., Lowney, G., Wallace, S., Reddi, V.J., Hazelwood, K.: Pin: building customized program analysis tools with dynamic instrumentation. SIGPLAN Not. 40, 190–200 (2005)
13. Nethercote, N., Seward, J.: Valgrind: a framework for heavyweight dynamic binary instrumentation. In: PLDI 2007, pp. 89–100. ACM (2007)
14. de Oliveira Stein, B., de Kergommeaux, J.C.: Pajé trace file format. Tech. rep. (March 2003)
15. Saha, B., Adl-Tabatabai, A.R., Hudson, R.L., Minh, C.C., Hertzberg, B.: Mcrt-stm: a high performance software transactional memory system for a multi-core runtime. In: PPoPP 2006, pp. 187–197. ACM, New York (2006)
16. Sonmez, N., Cristal, A., Unsal, O., Harris, T., Valero, M.: Profiling transactional memory applications on an atomic block basis: A haskell case study. In: MULTI-PROG 2009 (January 2009)
17. Wolf, F., Mohr, B.: Epilog binary trace-data format. Tech. rep., FZJ-ZAM-IB-2004-06 (May 2004)
18. Zyulkyarov, F., Stipic, S., Harris, T., Unsal, O.S., Cristal, A., Hur, I., Valero, M.: Discovering and understanding performance bottlenecks in transactional applications. In: PACT 2010, pp. 285–294. ACM, New York (2010)

A Comparison of the Influence of Different Multi-core Processors on the Runtime Overhead for Application-Level Monitoring

Jan Waller[1] and Wilhelm Hasselbring[1,2]

[1] Software Engineering Group, Christian-Albrechts-University Kiel, Germany
[2] SPEC Research Group, Steering Committee, Gainesville, VA, USA

Abstract. Application-level monitoring is required for continuously operating software systems to maintain their performance and availability at runtime. Performance monitoring of software systems requires storing time series data in a monitoring log or stream. Such monitoring may cause a significant runtime overhead to the monitored system.

In this paper, we evaluate the influence of multi-core processors on the overhead of the Kieker application-level monitoring framework. We present a breakdown of the monitoring overhead into three portions and the results of extensive controlled laboratory experiments with micro-benchmarks to quantify these portions of monitoring overhead under controlled and repeatable conditions. Our experiments show that the already low overhead of the Kieker framework may be further reduced on multi-core processors with asynchronous writing of the monitoring log.

Our experiment code and data are available as open source software such that interested researchers may repeat or extend our experiments for comparison on other hardware platforms or with other monitoring frameworks.

1   Introduction

Through the advent of multi-core processors in the consumer market, parallel systems became a commodity [12]. The semiconductor industry today is relying on adding cores, introducing hyper-threading, and putting several processors on the motherboard to increase the performance, since physical limitations impede further performance gains based on increasing clock speed. A fundamental question is how to exploit these emerging hardware architectures for software applications. Parallel programming languages intend to offer the programmer features for explicit parallel programming, while parallelizing compilers try to detect implicit concurrency in sequential programs for parallel execution. In this paper, we report on our research for exploiting parallel hardware for monitoring software systems.

In addition to studying the construction and evolution of software systems, the software engineering discipline needs to address the *operation* of continuously running software systems. A requirement for the robust operation of software

V. Pankratius and M. Philippsen (Eds.): MSEPT 2012, LNCS 7303, pp. 42–53, 2012.

systems are means for effective monitoring of the software's runtime behavior. In contrast to profiling for construction activities, monitoring of operational services should impose only a small performance overhead [5].

Various approaches attempt to reduce the overhead of monitoring large software systems. Self-adaptive monitoring approaches start with a comprehensively instrumented system and reduce the monitoring coverage through rule-based (de-)activation of selected probes at runtime [3, 10, 17]. [4] demonstrate the feasibility of this approach, given that the remaining overhead of deactivated probes is negligible. Another approach to reducing the overhead of monitoring is a reduction of the amount of data written with each monitoring record. Instead of using human readable file formats (e.g. XML, CSV, or ASCII), binary files provide an efficient storage of monitoring data. [2], for instance, integrate a compression algorithm to reduce the amount of log data. This compression could either be handled by a spare processor core or by using generally available free CPU resources in enterprise systems.

Our complementary idea is to use (potentially) underutilized processing units (processors, cores, hyper-threads) for further reducing the overhead of collecting monitoring data. To evaluate our approach of exploiting parallel hardware for monitoring software systems with the Kieker[1] framework and to determine the positive or negative (e.g., higher overhead of communication) influence of multiple available processing units we use benchmarks. As discussed by [21], benchmarks are an effective and affordable way of conducting experiments in computer science. As [6] state, benchmarking is at the heart of experimental computer science and research.

As contribution of this paper, we present a breakdown of the Kieker monitoring overhead into three portions and the results of extensive micro-benchmarks on various multi-core processor configurations with application-level monitoring tools on the example of the Kieker framework for application monitoring and dynamic software analysis [9].

A major result is a quantification of the individual portions of monitoring overhead, the identification of the main sources of overhead, and the proof that for asynchronous monitoring writers with the Kieker framework, the availability of (idle) processing units (processors, cores, hyper-threads) significantly reduces the (already very low) overhead of monitoring software applications. Thus, we show that multi-core processors may effectively be exploited to reduce the runtime overhead of monitoring software systems with Kieker. The micro-benchmarks available with our releases of Kieker can be applied to other monitoring frameworks and on other hardware platforms.

The remainder of this paper is organized as follows. Section 2 provides a brief overview of the Kieker framework. Section 3 introduces a partition of monitoring overhead into three portions. Section 4 presents the results of three different micro-benchmarks with the Kieker framework to quantify these portions of overhead in different scenarios. Section 5 discusses related work. Finally, Section 6 draws our conclusions and indicates areas for future research.

---

[1] http://kieker-monitoring.net

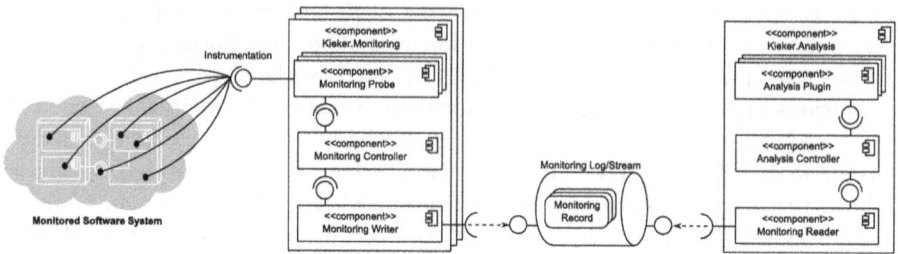

Fig. 1. Top-level view on the Kieker framework architecture

2   Overview on the Kieker Framework

The Kieker framework [8, 9] is an extensible framework for monitoring and analyzing the runtime behavior of concurrent or distributed software systems. It
provides components for software instrumentation, collection of information, logging of collected data, and analysis/visualization of monitoring data. Each Kieker
component is extensible and replaceable to support specific project contexts. A
top-level view on the Kieker framework architecture and its components is presented in Figure 1.

In this paper, we focus on the Kieker.Monitoring component to monitor software
systems. This configuration allows for the insertion of Monitoring Probes into the
Monitored Software System, e.g., instrumenting methods with probe code. With any
execution of the monitored (instrumented) methods, these probes collect data and
store it in Monitoring Records. The Monitoring Controller coordinates the activation
and deactivation of Monitoring Probes and connects the probes with the single Monitoring Writer. This writer receives the records and forwards them to the Monitoring
Log/Stream, e.g., a file system, a database, or a remote message queue connected
to a Monitoring Reader. A more detailed description of how method executions are
monitored is presented in Section 3.

The Monitoring Log/Stream acts as an interface between the Kieker.Monitoring
and the Kieker.Analysis component, facilitating both online and offline analyses.

The Kieker.Analysis component consists of an Analysis Controller component that
instructs the Monitoring Reader to retrieve Monitoring Records from the Monitoring Log/Stream enabling a series of Analysis Plugins to analyze and visualize the
recorded data. Some Analysis Plugins available with the Kieker framework support the reconstruction of traces, the automated generation of UML sequence
diagrams, dependency graphs, and call graphs. Refer to [8, 9] for more information on analysis and visualization with Kieker.

Note that the execution of all the components of Kieker.Monitoring up to the
point of storing/transferring the Monitoring Record into the Monitoring Log/Stream
is in the same execution context as the Monitored Software System, i.e., its execution
time and access to other resources have to be shared with the Monitored Software
System. Thus, a low overhead is essential. In the following section, we take a close
look at the portions that contribute to this overhead.

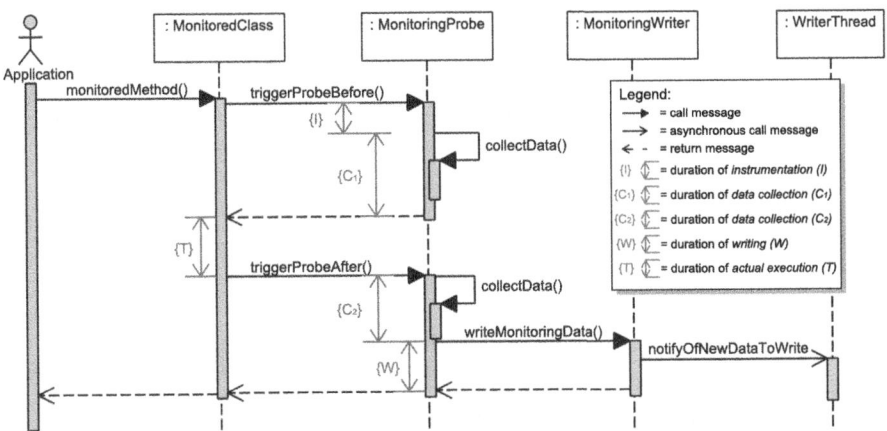

Fig. 2. UML sequence diagram for method monitoring with the Kieker framework

3   Portions of the Monitoring Overhead

A monitored software system has to share some of its resources (e.g., CPU time or memory) with the monitoring framework. In Figure 2, we present a UML sequence diagram representation of the control flow for monitoring a method execution. With a typical monitoring framework, such as Kieker, there are three possible causes of overhead while monitoring an application:

I   Before the code of the monitoredMethod() in the MonitoredClass is executed, the triggerProbeBefore() part of the MonitoringProbe is executed. Within the probe, it is determined whether monitoring is activated or deactivated for the monitoredMethod(). If monitoring is deactivated, no further probe code will be executed and the control flow immediately returns to the monitoredMethod().

C   The probe will collect some initial data during C_1 (in main memory), such as the current time and the operation signature before returning the control flow to the monitoredMethod(). When the execution of the actual code of the monitoredMethod() is finished with activated monitoring, the trigger-ProbeAfter() part of the MonitoringProbe is executed. Again, some additional data is collected during C_2 (in main memory), such as the response time or the return values of the monitored method. ($C = C_1 + C_2$)

W   Finally, writeMonitoringData() forwards the collected data to the Monitoring-Writer. The MonitoringWriter either stores the collected data in an internal buffer, that is processed asynchronously by a WriterThread into a Monitoring Log/Stream, or it synchronously writes the collected data by itself into the Monitoring Log/Stream. Here, only asynchronous writing is illustrated.

To sum up, in addition to the normal execution time of the monitoredMethod() T, there are three possible portions of overhead: (1) the instrumentation of the method and the check for activation of the probe (I), (2) the collection of data (C), and (3) the writing of collected data (W).

4 Micro-benchmarks with Kieker

In order to determine these three portions of monitoring overhead, we perform a
series of micro-benchmarks designed to determine the overhead of each individual
portion. These experiments are performed with the Kieker framework, but any
typical application-level monitoring framework should produce similar results.
A detailed description of the used benchmarks will be published later.

First, we document the configuration of the experiment (Section 4.1). Then,
we describe benchmarks to measure the influence of available cores (Section 4.2),
to determine the linear scalability of the Kieker framework (Section 4.3), and to
compare the influence of different multi-core platforms (Section 4.4).

4.1 Micro-benchmark Configuration

The micro-benchmark used in our experiments is designed to measure the three
individual portions of monitoring overhead. In order to allow an easy repeata-
bility, all necessary parts of the benchmark are included in releases of Kieker.

Each experiment consists of four independent runs. Each individual portion of
the execution time is measured by one run (see T, I, C, and W in Figure 2). In
the first run, only the execution time of the monitoredMethod() is determined (T).
In the second run, the monitoredMethod() is instrumented with a Monitoring Probe,
that is deactivated for the monitoredMethod(). Thus, the duration $T + I$ is measured. The third run adds the data collection with an activated Monitoring Probe
without writing any collected data $(T + I + C)$. The fourth run finally represents the measurement of full monitoring with the addition of an active Monitoring Writer and possibly an active Writer Thread $(T + I + C + W)$. This way, we
can incrementally measure the different portions of monitoring overhead.

We utilize a typical enterprise server machine for our experiments, in this case
a X6270 Blade Server with two Intel Xeon 2.53 GHz E5540 Quadcore processors
and 24 GB RAM running Solaris 10 and an Oracle Java 64-bit Server VM in
version 1.6.0_26 with 1 GB of heap space. We use Kieker release 1.4 as the Monitoring component. AspectJ release 1.6.12 with load-time weaving is used to insert
the particular Monitoring Probes into the Java bytecode. As mentioned before, the
Kieker framework can easily be replaced by another monitoring framework to
compare our benchmark results with results of similar frameworks.

We repeat the experiments on ten identically configured JVM instances, calling the monitoredMethod() 2,000,000 times on each run with an execution time
of 500 μs per method call. We discard the first 1,000,000 measured executions
as the warm-up period and use the second 1,000,000 steady state executions to
determine our results.

In this configuration, each experiment consists of four independent runs and
each run takes a total time of 20 minutes. Each run with an active Monitoring
Writer produces at least 362 MB of Kieker monitoring log files.

We perform our benchmarks under controlled conditions in our software performance engineering lab that is exclusively used for the experiments. Aside from
the experiment, the server machine is held idle and is not utilized.

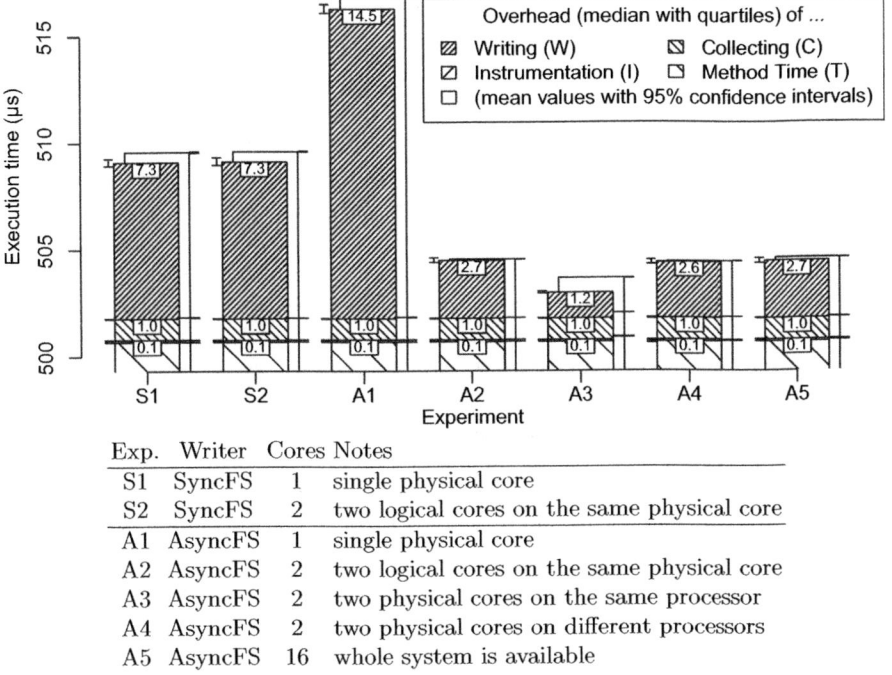

Exp.	Writer	Cores	Notes
S1	SyncFS	1	single physical core
S2	SyncFS	2	two logical cores on the same physical core
A1	AsyncFS	1	single physical core
A2	AsyncFS	2	two logical cores on the same physical core
A3	AsyncFS	2	two physical cores on the same processor
A4	AsyncFS	2	two physical cores on different processors
A5	AsyncFS	16	whole system is available

Fig. 3. Single-Threaded Monitoring Overhead

4.2 The Influence of Available Cores on the Monitoring Overhead

The focus of this series of experiments is to quantify the three portions of monitoring overhead and to measure the influence of different assignments of multiple cores or processors to the application (and to the Monitoring component) on the monitoring overhead. In order to achieve this goal, we are using operating system commands to assign only a subset of the available cores to the monitored application and to the monitoring framework.[2] Our X6270 Blade Server contains two processors, each processor consists of four cores, and each core is split into two logical cores via hyper-threading. The assignment of cores is documented in Figure 3.

The configuration of all experiments in this section is as specified in Section 4.1. The Monitoring Writer that is used by the Monitoring component during the measurement of the portion W of the overhead is either the Kieker asynchronous file system writer (AsyncFS) or the Kieker synchronous file system writer (SyncFS).

The results of the experiments are presented in Figure 3 and described below.

---

[2] On our Solaris 10 server we use the psrset command. Similar commands are available on other operating systems.

S1 We start our series of experiments with a synchronous file system Monitoring-Writer, thus disabling the internal buffer and the asynchronous WriterThread, yielding a single-threaded benchmark system. First, we assign a single physical core to the application and disable its second logical core, thus simulating a single core system. The main portion of overhead in S1 is generated by the writer W (7.3 µs), that has to share its execution time with the monitored application. The overhead of the instrumentation I is negligible (0.1 µs), the overhead of the data collection C is low (1.0 µs).

S2 In Experiment S2 we activate two logical cores (hyper-threading) in a single physical core and repeat the experiment with the synchronous writer. There is no significant difference between one or two assigned cores. For this reason we omit further synchronous experiments. Only with asynchronous writing, multiple processing units may reduce the monitoring overhead.

A1 We continue the rest of our series of experiments with the asynchronous file system Monitoring Writer. Similar to experiment S1, we assign a single physical core to the application and disable its second logical core. The portion W of the overhead caused by the writer (14.5 µs) is almost doubled compared to the synchronous writer. This can be explained by the writer thread sharing its execution time with the monitored application. Compared to the experiment S1, context switches and synchronization between the two active threads degrade the performance of the system.

A2 Next, we activate two logical cores in a single physical core. The additional core has no measurable influence on the overhead of instrumentation I (0.1 µs) and collecting data C (1.0 µs). Due to the additional available core, which is exclusively used by the writer thread, the overhead of writing the data W (2.7 µs) is significantly reduced. Even though both logical cores have to share the resources of a single physical core, the second logical core proofed to be an enormous improvement. The overhead could be reduced by 55% of the overhead of the synchronous writer (S1) and by 76% of the overhead of the single core system with the asynchronous writer (A1).

A3 In this experiment we assign two different physical cores on the same processor to the benchmark system. This setup provides the best results of the series of experiments with again greatly improved writer performance W (1.2 µs). The improvement can be explained by no longer sharing the processing resources of a single physical core by two logical cores (via hyper-threading). Thus, the overhead of monitoring could be reduced by 73% of the overhead of the synchronous writer (S1) and by 85% of the overhead of the single core system with the asynchronous writer (A1).

A4 Next, we assign two physical cores of two different processors on the motherboard. The increased synchronization overhead between two different processors causes results similar to A2.

A5 Finally, we activate all physical and logical cores in the system. Since the monitored software system uses a single thread and the monitoring framework uses an additional writer thread, no additional benefit of more than two available cores is measurable: the two threads (one for the application and one for monitoring) cannot exploit more than two cores.

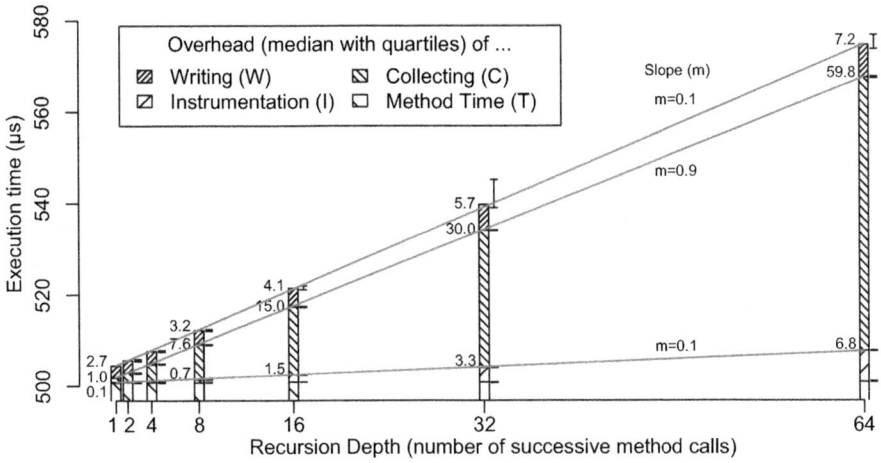

Fig. 4. Linear Increase of Monitoring Overhead

4.3   The Scalability of Monitoring Overhead

Only a linear increase of monitoring overhead is acceptable for good scalability. In order to determine whether the increase of the amount of monitoring overhead with each additional monitored method call is linear, we perform a series of experiments with increasing recursion depths. Thus, in each experiment run, each call of the monitoredMethod() results in additional recursive (monitored) calls of this method, enabling us to measure the overhead of monitoring multiple successive method calls. The benchmarks are performed with the Kieker asynchronous file system writer (AsyncFS) in a configuration similar to the one described in experiment A5 in the previous section. Apart from the increasing recursion depths, the configuration of the experiment is as described previously.

The results of this experiment are presented in Figure 4 and described below.

The measured overhead of instrumentation I increases with a constant value of approximately 0.1 µs per call. The overhead of collecting data C increases with a constant value of approximately 0.9 µs per call. The overhead of writing W consists of two parts: a constant overhead of approximately 2.5 µs during the period of 500 µs and an increasing value of approximately 0.1 µs per additional call.

Our experiments include recursion depths up to 64 method calls per 500 µs. With higher values of the recursion depth, the monitoring system records method calls faster than it is able to store monitoring records in the file system.

In each experiment run, the Monitoring Writer has to process 362 MB of monitoring log data per step of recursion depth. In the case of a recursion depth of 64, 23 GB Kieker monitoring log data were processed and written to disk within the 20 minutes execution time (at 19.3 MB/s).

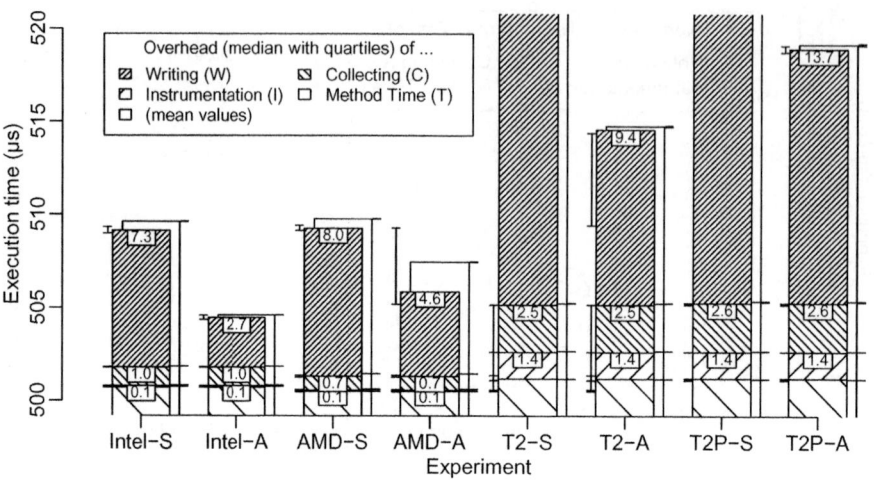

Fig. 5. A comparison of different multi-core architectures

4.4   The Influence of Different Multi-core Architectures

In this final experiment, we compare the results of our benchmarks on several different multi-core architectures with each other. The goal of this experiment is a generalization of our results in the previous sections.

Besides the X6270 Blade server with two Intel Xeon E5540 (Intel), we use a X6240 Blade with two AMD Opteron 2384 2.7 GHz processors (AMD), a T6330 Blade with two Sun UltraSparc 1.4 GHz T2 processors (T2), and a T6340 Blade with two Sun UltraSparc 1.4 GHz T2+ processors (T2P).

On each server, we compare two different benchmark runs. The first run is performed with a synchronous writer (S) and is similar to S2 in Section 4.2. The second run is performed with an asynchronous writer (A) and corresponds to experiment A5. The results of these experiments are presented in Figure 5 and are described below.

Compared to our Intel experiments, the AMD architecture provides slightly improved performance in the collecting portion C with a similar performance of the synchronous writer while the performance gain of the asynchronous writer is slightly worse. The Sun UltraSparc architectures provide lots of slower logical cores (64 on the T2, 128 on the T2+) compared to the Intel or AMD architectures. The result is a significant increase of the monitoring overhead. Yet, an asynchronous writer provides an even greater benefit compared to a synchronous writer. In the case of the T2 processor, the overhead of writing W is reduced from 69.4 μs to 9.4 μs. In the case of the T2+ processor, the overhead is reduced from 64.9 μs to 13.7 μs.

In all experiments, the writing portion W of the overhead can be greatly reduced with the usage of an asynchronous monitoring writer and available cores.

5   Related Work

In this section, we compare related approaches to exploiting multiple cores to reduce the runtime overhead for monitoring software systems.

One approach is the usage of additional specialized hardware mechanisms to reduce the overhead of profiling, monitoring, or analysis of software systems [2, 16]. Contrary to this, our goal with the Kieker framework is to build a software-based, portable framework for application performance monitoring that imposes only a very small overhead to the monitored application, particularly via exploiting multi-core processors. Furthermore, additional cores reserved or used for monitoring are comparable to dedicated profiling hardware.

Several authors [15, 19, 23] propose shadow processes, i.e., instrumented clones of actual parts of the monitored system, running on spare cores, thus minimizing influence on the execution of the main system. The goal of application-level monitoring is recording the actual events in the system, including any side effects, while keeping the overhead and the influence of monitoring minimal. Furthermore, cloning is usually not viable for interactive enterprise systems.

Another possibility is the separation of monitoring and analysis [2, 7, 24] in order to either execute the analysis concurrently on another core or to delegate it to specialized hardware. This is the usual approach in application-level monitoring and also employed by Kieker.

Most of these related works apply to profilers and fine-grained monitoring solutions. In the field of application-level performance monitoring, most performance evaluations are far less sophisticated. Despite the fact that reports on monitoring frameworks often include an overhead evaluation, a detailed description of the experimental design and a detailed analysis of the results, including confidence intervals, is often missing (see for instance [1, 11, 13, 14, 18, 22]).

6   Conclusion and Future Work

Multi-core processors may effectively be exploited to reduce the runtime overhead of monitoring software systems on the application level. To evaluate whether monitoring frameworks are really able to use available processing units (processors, cores, hyper-threads) for reducing the overhead of collecting monitoring data, we proposed a splitting of monitoring overhead in three portions and designed a micro-benchmark with a series of experiments to quantify these various portions of monitoring overhead under controlled and repeatable conditions.

Extensive micro-benchmarks were performed with the Kieker framework and the results are presented in this paper. For asynchronous monitoring writers, the availability of (idle) processing units may significantly reduce the (already very low) overhead of monitoring software applications with the Kieker framework.

The benchmarks may be applied to other monitoring frameworks and on other hardware platforms. So far, we performed our experiments on multiple hardware platforms with a specific operating system and a specific Java virtual machine. Other combinations of hardware, operating system and virtual machines may yield other results. Thus, we intend to validate the presented results on other platforms that are available in our software performance engineering lab. Further experiments can be performed to determine the exact assignment of processing units to active threads within the monitoring framework. Thus, a more detailed analysis of possible contention as a new source of overhead is possible. Additionally, the benchmarks might be adapted to other monitoring concepts, such as event based monitoring, that support a wider range of possible applications. Since, our experiment code and data are available as open source, interested researchers may repeat or extend our experiments for comparison on other hardware platforms or with other application-level monitoring frameworks.

According to [20], our benchmarks are so-called proto-benchmarks since benchmarks require a community that defines and uses its benchmarks. Such a community does not, as yet, exist. However, our intention is that interested researchers may repeat or extend our experiments for comparison. The Software Engineering Group of the University of Kiel is a member of the SPEC Research Group (http://research.spec.org/). We share Kieker and our monitoring benchmarks with this group and with other research groups that use Kieker [17, 25] as a start for community building.

References

[1] Chawla, A., Orso, A.: A generic instrumentation framework for collecting dynamic information. ACM SIGSOFT Softw. Eng. Notes 29, 1–4 (2004)
[2] Chen, S., Gibbons, P.B., Kozuch, M., Mowry, T.C.: Log-based architectures: Using multicore to help software behave correctly. ACM SIGOPS Operating Systems Review 45, 84–91 (2011)
[3] Ehlers, J., Hasselbring, W.: A Self-adaptive Monitoring Framework for Component-Based Software Systems. In: Crnkovic, I., Gruhn, V., Book, M. (eds.) ECSA 2011. LNCS, vol. 6903, pp. 278–286. Springer, Heidelberg (2011)
[4] Ehlers, J., van Hoorn, A., Waller, J., Hasselbring, W.: Self-adaptive software system monitoring for performance anomaly localization. In: Proc. of the 8th IEEE/ACM Int. Conf. on Autonomic Computing (ICAC 2011), pp. 197–200. ACM (2011)
[5] Gao, J., Zhu, E., Shim, S., Chang, L.: Monitoring software components and component-based software. In: The 24th Annual International Computer Software and Applications Conference (COMPSAC 2000), pp. 403–412. IEEE Computer Society (2000)
[6] Georges, A., Buytaert, D., Eeckhout, L.: Statistically rigorous Java performance evaluation. ACM SIGPLAN Notices 42, 57–76 (2007)
[7] Ha, J., Arnold, M., Blackburn, S., McKinley, K.: A concurrent dynamic analysis framework for multicore hardware. ACM SIGP. 44, 155–174 (2009)
[8] van Hoorn, A., Rohr, M., Hasselbring, W., Waller, J., Ehlers, J., Frey, S., Kieselhorst, D.: Continuous monitoring of software services: Design and application of the Kieker framework. Tech. Rep. TR-0921, Department of Computer Science, University of Kiel, Germany (2009)
[9] van Hoorn, A., Waller, J., Hasselbring, W.: Kieker: A framework for application performance monitoring and dynamic software analysis. In: Proc. of 3rd ACM/SPEC Int. Conf. on Performance Eng. (ICPE 2012). ACM (2012)

[10] Huang, X., Seyster, J., Callanan, S., Dixit, K., Grosu, R., Smolka, S., Stoller, S., Zadok, E.: Software monitoring with controllable overhead. Int. Journal on Software Tools for Technology Transfer (STTT), 1–21 (2010)

[11] Maebe, J., Buytaert, D., Eeckhout, L., De Bosschere, K.: Javana: A system for building customized Java program analysis tools. ACM SIGPLAN Notices 41, 153–168 (2006)

[12] Marowka, A.: Parallel computing on any desktop. Communications of the ACM 50, 74–78 (2007)

[13] Moon, S., Chang, B.M.: A thread monitoring system for multithreaded Java programs. ACM SIGPLAN Notices 41, 21–29 (2006)

[14] Mos, A.: A Framework for Adaptive Monitoring and Performance Management of Component-Based Enterprise Applications. Ph.D. thesis, Dublin City University (2004)

[15] Moseley, T., Shye, A., Reddi, V.J., Grunwald, D., Peri, R.: Shadow profiling: Hiding instrumentation costs with parallelism. In: Int. Symp. on Code Generation and Optimization (CGO 2007), pp. 198–208 (2007)

[16] Nair, A., Shankar, K., Lysecky, R.: Efficient hardware-based nonintrusive dynamic application profiling. ACM Transactions on Embedded Computing Systems 10, 32:1–32:22 (2011)

[17] Okanović, D., van Hoorn, A., Konjović, Z., Vidaković, M.: Towards adaptive monitoring of Java EE applications. In: Proc. of the 5th Int. Conf. on Information Technology (ICIT 2011). IEEE Computer Society (2011)

[18] Parsons, T., Mos, A., Murphy, J.: Non-intrusive end-to-end runtime path tracing for J2EE systems. IEEE Software 153, 149–161 (2006)

[19] Patil, H., Fischer, C.N.: Efficient run-time monitoring using shadow processing. In: AADEBUG, pp. 119–132 (1995)

[20] Sim, S.E., Easterbrook, S., Holt, R.C.: Using benchmarking to advance research: A challenge to software engineering. In: Proc. of the 25th Int. Conf. on Software Engineering (ICSE 2003), pp. 74–83. IEEE (2003)

[21] Tichy, W.: Should computer scientists experiment more? IEEE Computer 31, 32–40 (1998)

[22] Vlachos, E., Goodstein, M.L., Kozuch, M., Chen, S., Falsafi, B., Gibbons, P., Mowry, T.: ParaLog: Enabling and accelerating online parallel monitoring of multithreaded applications. ACM SIGPLAN Notices 45, 271–284 (2010)

[23] Wallace, S., Hazelwood, K.: SuperPin: Parallelizing dynamic instrumentation for real-time performance. In: Int. Symp. on Code Generation and Optimization (CGO 2007), pp. 209–220 (2007)

[24] Zhao, Q., Cutcutache, I., Wong, W.F.: Pipa: Pipelined profiling and analysis on multi-core systems. In: Proc. of the 6th Annual IEEE/ACM Int. Symp. on Code Generation and Optimization (CGO 2008), pp. 185–194. ACM (2008)

[25] Zheng, Q., Ou, Z., Liu, L., Liu, T.: A novel method on software structure evaluation. In: Proc. of the 2nd IEEE Int. Conf. on Software Engineering and Service (ICSESS 2011). IEEE Computer Society (2011)

Analysis of Event Processing Design Patterns and Their Performance Dependency on I/O Notification Mechanisms

Ronald Strebelow and Christian Prehofer

Fraunhofer Institute for Communication Systems ESK, Munich, Germany

Abstract. Software design patterns reflect software engineering practices and experience by documenting proven design solutions. We consider here two widely used patterns, the Half-Sync/Half-Async and the Leader/Followers pattern, which aim for efficient processing of messages in multi-core environments.

We will analyze the performance differences not only between both design patterns but also between different implementation variants. These variants use different event notification mechanisms which are used to sense message arrivals on a set of connections. We will show that performance depends not simply on data sharing or lock contention but on the selected event notification primitives and their specific characteristics.

In more detail, we evaluated both patterns in terms of three different event notification mechanisms: `select`, level-triggered and edge-triggered `epoll`. The latter two are the operation modes of the `epoll` API. In particular, the right choice of the API can influence the performance by a factor of two. Secondly, the more recent `epoll` is overall faster, but in some aspects slower which strongly degrades the Half-Sync/Half-Async performance. Existing performance evaluations for these patterns do not analyze their multi-core performance. Furthermore, they do not include analysis of bottlenecks, data sharing, or operating system primitives.

1   Introduction

It is well known that designing efficient concurrent software is a challenging task. Software design patterns can help in this process. They are created through careful analysis of existing software and capture designs that have been proven useful and have been used in many different systems. These design patterns then aid developers by providing extensive experience.

We consider the problem of handling messages from a large number of input streams on multiple cores of a single machine. There exist several design patterns that aim to solve this problem. For this paper we choose two of the most prominent ones, namely Half-Sync/Half-Async and Leader/Followers.

The Half-Sync/Half-Async pattern is widely used. It is used in the implementations of network stacks of most operating systems [12]. The work in [3] found the pattern in 3 of 21 analyzed legacy software systems and their documentations. Both Half-Sync/Half-Async and Leader/Followers are also used in multi-threaded implementations of OMG's CORBA [2,7,9,13].

V. Pankratius and M. Philippsen (Eds.): MSEPT 2012, LNCS 7303, pp. 54–65, 2012.

Both patterns differ mainly in their distribution of tasks to threads. For instance, the Leader/Followers pattern uses a pool of identical threads which have to synchronize their access to the input streams. In contrast, Half-Sync/Half-Async has a pipeline-architecture. It uses a dedicated thread to retrieve incoming messages and forwards them to the remaining threads which process these messages.

The performance of both patterns does not solely depend on their architecture, i.e., usage of locks or sharing of data, but also on I/O notification mechanisms for new messages. For this, different approaches exist: thread-based approaches, i.e., using one thread per connection and blocking receive and send operations, and event-based ones which are divided into asynchronous, e.g., notification via signals, and synchronous. This last approach groups all connections into a so-called interest set and retrieves new events through a single blocking, i.e., synchronous, system call. This is the most commonly used approach and utilized by Half-Sync/Half-Async and Leader/Followers. In our paper, we analyze two API's implementing this approach: `select` and the more recent `epoll`. The latter was designed to scale to large amounts of connections. Discussion, e.g., in [1,6,8], and the fact that current software, e.g., Apache HTTP Server[1], Kamailio[2] (former OpenSER), or SQUID[3], use `epoll` if available confirmed the achievement of that goal. Here, we are interested in the scalability in terms of number of threads rather than connections.

Our aim is to analyze the performance of the aforementioned design patterns in conjunction with the different event notification mechanisms. We will show that both design patterns have significantly different performance characteristics. And we will show that performance depends not only on data sharing or lock contention but on the event notification primitives selected and their specific characteristics.

Both, the software design patterns and the event notification mechanisms have been subject of evaluations before. These evaluations consider very specific applications like web servers[1,8] or CORBA [2,7,9,13]. These include operations which are unrelated to patterns or notification mechanisms but affect performance. Also, these benchmarks do not consider scalability but performance for a particular setup. These setups include only quad-core CPU's. Here, we evaluate performance and scalability for up to 16 cores. Our setup uses two comparable implementations of the patterns, which focus on the core problem.

2   I/O and Event Notification Mechanisms

In this section, we present the different event notification mechanisms which we used to implement the Half-Sync/Half-Async and Leader/Followers patterns.

There exist different ways to retrieve information about message arrival, summarized in [6]. One of these is thread-based, i.e., using one thread per connection

---

[1] httpd.apache.org

[2] www.kamailio.org

[3] www.squid-cache.org

or request. These threads retrieve information by reading from the connection, which will block until a message arrives. This approach requires many resources and, due to high over-subscription of available CPUs, causes frequent context switches. A second approach uses asynchronous event-based notification, e.g., via signals. [5,11] found this approach to be inferior to thread-based mechanisms, especially for small workloads. Another approach, synchronous event-based notification, is to group all connections into a so-called interest set. Instead of waiting for messages from a single connection, a specific synchronous system call is used to wait for messages on any connection that is contained in the interest set.

We used two common synchronous event notification mechanisms: Firstly, the `select` system call which is available on most operating systems. And secondly, the more recent `epoll`, a Linux specific API which provides two modes: level-triggered and edge-triggered. All three mechanisms are summarized in the following:

select. The `select` API maintains the interest set, actually a bit set, in user space. On each invocation that set is copied into kernel-space. `select` does not return occurred events for a connection but the state of the same. Thus, it does not report incoming messages but that data is available for reading.

epoll. The `epoll` API maintains the interest set in kernel-space using a red-black tree. Unlike `select`, an invocation returns a sub-set of the interest set, such that idle connections are omitted. This makes `epoll` suitable for big sets with a high number of idle connections.

    level-triggered. This mode behaves much like `select` since it returns the state of a connection instead of events. Multi-threaded software has to avoid that a connection is falsely reported several times to have data available. For this purpose it is possible to deactivate a connection automatically. Once a connection is deactivated it has to be reactivated explicitly using another system call.

    edge-triggered. In this mode, `epoll` does indeed return occurred events and the software is required to manage connection state which hinders programming. Since only new events are reported, it is not necessary to de- and reactivate connections. This saves a system call per event and may provide for better performance.

3   Design Patterns

In this section we briefly introduce the Half-Sync/Half-Async and the Leader/ Followers pattern. For a detailed description including both patterns we refer to [10].

3.1   Half-Sync/Half-Async

The Half-Sync/Half-Async pattern provides parallelism by executing different services in different threads. These services may communicate with each other by utilizing a central queue and are divided into two groups:

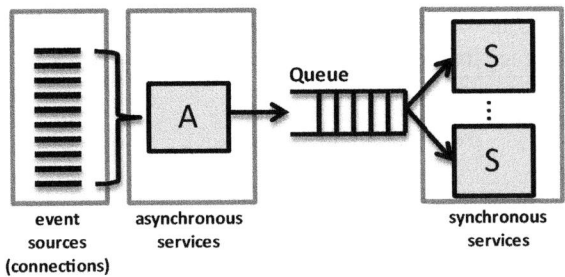

Fig. 1. Components of the Half-Sync/Half-Async pattern

Algorithm 1. Pseudo code of the asynchronous service

---

loop
    poll system for events

    for all event **do**
        push event into queue
    end for
end loop

Asynchronous services are triggered by events. These services can also process data read from the queue.

Synchronous services get their data from the queue exclusively. If no data is available these services wait for it to arrive.

Our implementation of Half-Sync/Half-Async, shown in Fig. 1, uses two kinds of services. The first one, an asynchronous service, multiplexes events from a set of event sources, indicating incoming messages. Each new event is inserted into the queue for further processing. This service utilizes one thread. That decision is motivated by the Leader/Followers pattern which has to synchronize its access to the set of connections. We will explain this in detail in the next section. To remain comparable only a single thread is allowed to multiplex these events. Apart from this, a multi-threaded asynchronous service is possible. The second service, a synchronous one, demultiplexes events from the queue to multiple threads which process them, one at a time. Processing essentially consists of reading the message, sending the response and, in case of level-triggered `epoll` and `select`, reactivation of the connection. Pseudo code for both services is shown in Alg. 1 and 2.

The access to the event sources is more subtle than shown in Fig. 1. The asynchronous service must access these to report any new events. The synchronous service on the other hand must access these when sending or receiving on the associated connection.

The pattern as shown above has three potential bottlenecks: the asynchronous service, the queue, and the synchronous service. The asynchronous service may

Algorithm 2. Pseudo code of the synchronous service; the code is executed by each of the multiple threads

loop
  pop event from queue

  read message
  reactivate connection
  process message
  send response
end loop

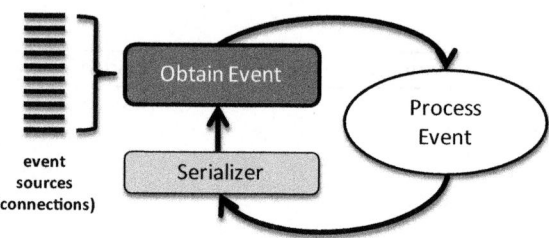

Fig. 2. Execution cycle each thread in the Leader/Followers pattern performs

bottleneck because of his single thread. If the thread reaches full utilization, the throughput reaches its maximum. The queue is a central resource protected by a mutex. If the number of threads is too high, lock contention is going to decrease overall performance. The threads of the synchronous service, especially in case of level-triggered `epoll`, have to perform connection reactivation. It includes a lock (in the kernel) which may be heavily contended.

3.2 Leader/Followers

The Leader/Followers pattern organizes its threads in a thread pool. All threads try to access the set of event sources and therefore must synchronize. To obtain an event one of the synchronous notification mechanisms are used and, if necessary, the connection is deactivated. Once a new event is obtained, it is processed by the same thread. Several threads may process distinct events in parallel. As was the the case for Half-Sync/Half-Async, processing consists of reading the message, sending the response and, in case of level-triggered `epoll` and `select`, reactivation of the connection. After processing has been finished the thread becomes idle and tries again to get access to the set of event sources. Figure 2 shows this cycle and Alg. 3 shows the pseudo code.

The performance of the Leader/Followers pattern is governed by a serial section in which the event notification mechanism is invoked. In our implementation serial access is enforced by a mutex.

Since all threads execute the same tasks they also have to share all data. In particular these are the state of the event sources and the data needed for any specific event notification mechanism.

Algorithm 3. Pseudo code of the work that each thread in the Leader/Followers pattern performs

---

loop
    enter serial section
    poll system for one new event
    leave serial section

    read message that caused event
    reactivate connection
    process message
    send response
end loop

---

4   Evaluation Set-Up

For the evaluation, presented in Sect. 5, we use two measurement metrics to support our findings: throughput and the time required for certain operations. These metrics were not measured during a complete run. Instead, each run consists of 3 phases. The initialization phase, the measurement phase and the shutdown phase. The first and the last did not participate in measurements.

The steady-state throughput is measured in messages per second. For more detailed analysis we measured the service times of certain operations. Each particular measurement was run 5 times over a period of 5 minutes each. We present the mean value of these 5 runs. For the measurement of the service times an operation was surrounded by primitives returning the time difference in nano-second granularity.

For the evaluation we use a request-response micro-benchmark utilizing 512 TCP/IP connections lasting over an entire run. The client component sends for each connection at most one request at a time. Only when the reply was received a new request is send. To support high throughput the client maintains as many threads as CPU cores are assigned to it.

The evaluation was performed on an AMD Opteron 6134 system with 4 CPU's supporting 8 cores each, and clocked at 2.3GHz. As operating system we are using Linux with kernel-version 2.6.35. Client and server component are assigned to 2 CPUs each, hence each use up to 16 cores. The distribution was chosen so that CPU resources, e.g., caches or the memory bus, are not shared between both components.

For the evaluation the Leader/Followers pattern was run with 1 to 16 threads and Half-Sync/Half-Async with 2 to 16 threads, since that pattern requires at least two threads.

Message processing consists of reading the message, performing a simulated workload through busy waiting a defined duration, and sending a response. Throughout Sect. 5 we assume that this workload takes $0\mu s$.

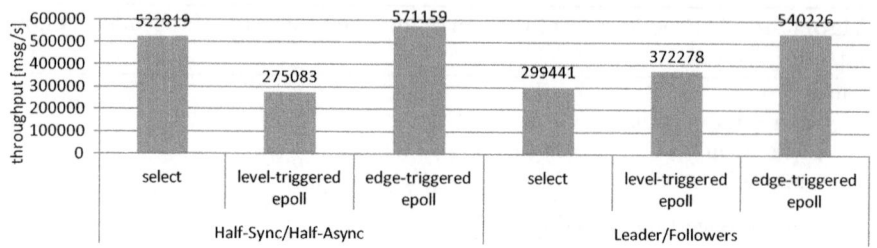

Fig. 3. Steady-state throughput of the Half-Sync/Half-Async and Leader/Followers patterns; both patterns are shown with their three implementation variants: select, level-triggered epoll, and edge-triggered epoll

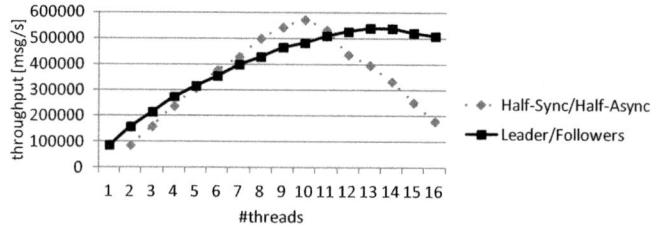

Fig. 4. Scaling of Half-Sync/Half-Async and Leader/Followers (both edge-triggered epoll) over increasing numbers of threads

5   Evaluation Results

In the following, we discuss the main results of our evaluation, comparing the two patterns and APIs in detail.

Figure 3 shows the steady-state throughput of both patterns and all event notification mechanisms described in Sect. 2. In the best case, i.e., using edge-triggered `epoll`, the Half-Sync/Half-Async pattern outperforms the Leader/Followers pattern. Figure 4 also shows that this is achieved with 10 instead of 13 threads. However, beyond 11 threads Leader/Followers shows better performance, as the Half-Sync/Half-Async has significant performance loss if too many cores are used.

5.1   Half-Sync/Half-Async

The Half-Sync/Half-Async pattern consists of a two-staged pipeline: The first stage is the asynchronous service and the second stage is the synchronous one. Thus, best performance is achieved if both services are fully utilized and perform equally fast.

In case of edge-triggered `epoll` and `select`, both services are fully utilized if the synchronous service uses 9 threads (Fig. 5), i.e., 10 threads are used overall. Using fewer threads causes an under-utilization of the asynchronous service.

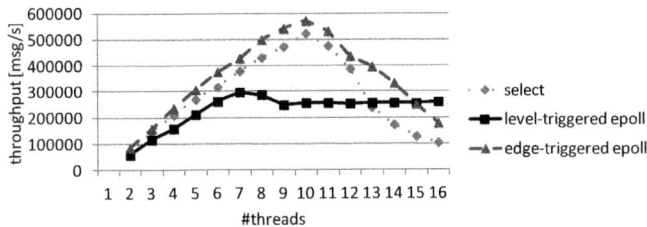

Fig. 5. Half-Sync/Half-Async: Throughput comparison of all three notification mechanisms

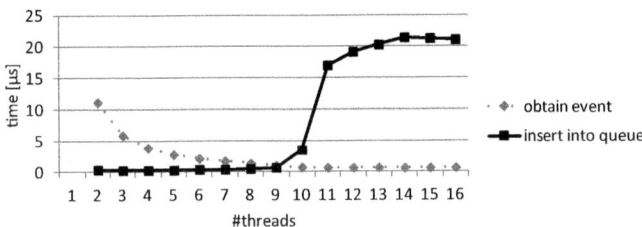

Fig. 6. Half-Sync/Half-Async (edge-triggered epoll): Average required time to obtain one event and to insert it into the queue

Figure 6 shows the time which is required to obtain a new event and the time it takes to put it into the queue. For small numbers of threads the asynchronous service spends its time waiting on new events, i.e., incoming messages. Adding threads to the synchronous service increases processing rate and in turn increases the number of overall messages in our benchmark system. This increased rate is observable through the reduced time spent for waiting. This rate is decreasing with the same rate as threads are added to the synchronous service.

The gap between the peak performance of the `select`- and the edge-triggered `epoll`-based implementation is caused by differences in the API's. Since `select` maintains its interest set in the user space, that set is required as parameter to the call. The same parameter is used to return the desired information and is therefore altered in place. This has to effects: On the one hand, a copy of the interest set is required instead of the original one. One the other hand, since the interest set is a bit set, the returned set has to be scanned for the desired information. In the worst case, the entire set contains only one event indication. We evaluated the number of events returned in average. We found that, in case of Half-Sync/Half-Async, no more than 8 such events are reported. In contrast, `epoll` omits the copy and also requires no scan since all returned elements indicate events.

The case of level-triggered `epoll` requires a more detailed analysis: Figure 7 shows the time it takes to process a single message and breaks that time down

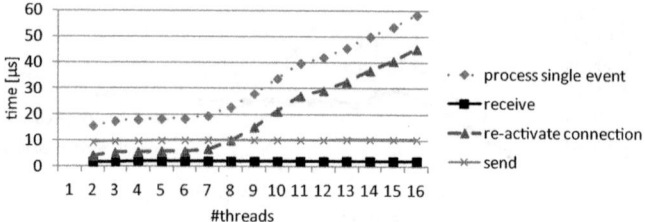

Fig. 7. Half-Sync/Half-Async (level-triggered epoll): Time required to process a single event, split into its basic operations receive, re-activate (connection), and send (a response)

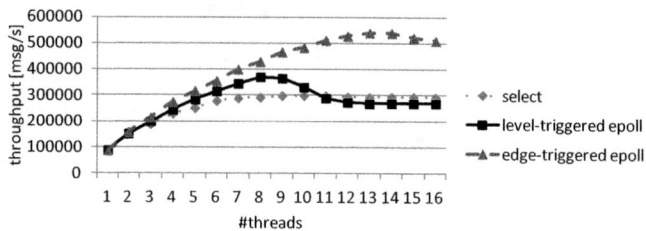

Fig. 8. Leader/Followers: Throughput comparison of all three notification mechanisms

into the three operations reception, connection re-activation, and transmission of the response.

Connection deactivation is needed for `select` and level-triggered `epoll` to avoid that new messages are reported several times. Deactivation is performed automatically without performance loss and we do not consider it here. Re-activation, after reading data, is necessary to receive the next message on one socket: `select` atomically sets the bit in the interest set which belongs to the connection. Level-triggered `epoll`, on the other hand, requires a system call. In the Linux kernel, the `epoll` API then searches the connection within a red-black tree and makes it available for subsequent calls. Afterwards it checks if events are already available and sets a specific flag in the control structure. Both operations are part of a serial section which is guarded by a lock. As Fig. 7 shows, the cost of these operations increase with the number of threads which inhibits a further increase of overall throughput.

5.2   Leader/Followers

The performance of the Leader/Followers pattern is limited by the serial section in which the set of event sources is accessed. Thus, there is a sweet spot at which the time required to process a message divided by the number of threads equals the time required to perform the serial section. Adding more threads does not increase performance.

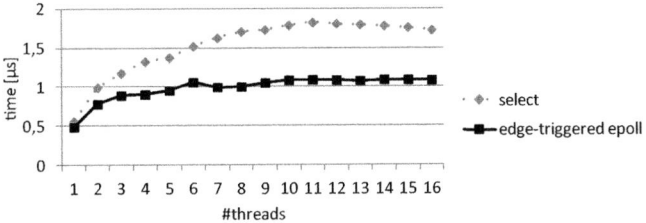

Fig. 9. Leader/Followers: Average time it takes to sense a single event using select or edge-triggered epoll

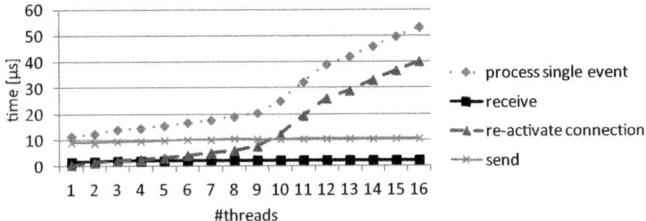

Fig. 10. Leader/Followers (level-triggered epoll): Time required to process a single event split into its basic operations receive, re-activate (connection), and send (a response)

Figure 8 shows the throughput achieved with each notification mechanism. The performance difference between the edge-triggered `epoll`- and the `select`-based implementation is striking. Also the graph of level-trigger `epoll` is peculiar. We will explain both peculiarities in the following:

Compared to Half-Sync/Half-Async the Leader/Followers pattern is more sensible for the efficiency of `select`. The Half-Sync/Half-Async pattern is not limited by its asynchronous service and hence, not limited by the efficiency of `select`. On the contrary, in case of Leader/Followers the lower performance of `select` takes effect (Fig. 9). Thus, on average a call to `select` needs almost 80% longer to complete than one to edge-triggered `epoll`. Hence, the serial section takes longer which causes a lower performance limit.

The case of level-triggered `epoll` is similar to that of the Half-Sync/Half-Async pattern. As Fig. 10 shows, the time required for processing a message increases as well. As before, this is again caused by connection re-activation. In consequence, increasing the number of threads compensates for the increased processing time but does not increase performance.

6   Related Work

In the existing literature, patterns and multi-threading strategies related to event handling are often implemented and evaluated in the context of OMG's

CORBA [2,7,9,13] and web servers [4,1,8]. In both cases Half-Sync/Half-Async and Leader/Followers are used to parallelize request processing.

Evaluation of performance is present in most of these papers but is performed on quad-core processors at best. Also benchmarks are affected by application-specific infrastructure. Only the work in [9] compares Half-Sync/Half-Async and Leader/Followers but does not provide any detailed analysis about the results. The authors found that Leader/Followers generally outperforms Half-Sync/Half-Async. Although not stated explicitly, the description of Half-Sync/Half-Async suggests that asynchronous operations are used for notification about incoming requests while `select` is used for Leader/Followers. In an earlier paper [4] the authors found that those asynchronous operations are efficient only for big messages of at least 50kByte.

In [1] `select` and `epoll` are evaluated in the context of userver[4] using dual-core Xeon system. In case of many idle connections, the authors found `epoll` to perform better than `select`. On the contrary, in case of few or no idle connections, both can perform equally well. Similar findings are presented in [8]. This paper uses a quad-core Xeon system but does not evaluate scalability. Both papers evaluated level-triggered `epoll` and used connection de- and reactivation. They consistently found that connection reactivation slowed down their benchmarks.

7   Conclusions

In this paper we evaluated the software design patterns Half-Sync/Half-Async and Leader/Followers. We implemented both patterns in terms of three different event notification mechanisms: `select`, level-triggered and edge-triggered `epoll`. The latter two are the operation modes of the `epoll` API.

In summary, we found that the performance of both patterns highly depends on the efficiency of the utilized API. We observed speed-ups up to a factor of two just by switching from `select` to edge-triggered `epoll`. Hence the developer of such patterns currently has to know the multi-core or parallel performance impact of the specific aspects of the patterns and APIs in order to obtain optimal performance.

The Leader/Followers pattern has lower peak performance but does not degrade as strongly as Half-Sync/Half-Async if too many cores are used. In practice, this means that the patterns should adapt the number of cores according to load.

Although `epoll` is generally faster, connection reactivation is slower than the corresponding `select` implementation. That is, the operation of reactivation is slower and in particular does not perform well for multi-core environments with many threads. In our case, this has led to the case that Half-Sync/Half-Async has performed better with `select` than with level-triggered `epoll`. The reason is that the reactivation is performed within the critical pipeline stage of this pattern. Hence, it causes performance loss.

---

[4] http://www.hpl.hp.com/research/linux/userver/

On the other hand, if the event notification mechanism is called within the critical path, as is the case for the Leader/Followers pattern, `select` is outperformed by `epoll`.

Acknowledgement. The work of Ronald Strebelow has been partially funded by Nokia Siemens Networks.

References

1. Gammo, L., Brecht, T., Shukla, A., Pariag, D.: Comparing and evaluating epoll, select, and poll event mechanisms. In: Proceedings of the Ottawa Linux Symposium (2004)
2. Harkema, M., Gijsen, B., van der Mei, R., Hoekstra, Y.: Middleware performance: A quantitative modeling approach (2004)
3. Harrison, N., Avgeriou, P.: Analysis of architecture pattern usage in legacy system architecture documentation. In: Seventh Working IEEE/IFIP Conference on Software Architecture, WICSA 2008, pp. 147–156 (2008)
4. Hu, J., Pyarali, I., Schmidt, D.: Measuring the impact of event dispatching and concurrency models on web server performance over high-speed networks. In: IEEE Global Telecommunications Conference, GLOBECOM 1997, vol. 3, pp. 1924–1931 (November 1997)
5. Hu, J., Pyarali, I., Schmidt, D.C.: Applying the proactor pattern to high-performance web servers. In: Proceedings of the 10th International Conference on Parallel and Distributed Computing and Systems (1998)
6. Kegel, D.: The c10k problem, http://www.kegel.com/c10k.html
7. Natarajan, B., Gokhale, A., Yajnik, S., Schmidt, D.C.: Applying Patterns to Improve the Performance of Fault Tolerant CORBA. In: Prasanna, V.K., Vajapeyam, S., Valero, M. (eds.) HiPC 2000. LNCS, vol. 1970, pp. 107–120. Springer, Heidelberg (2000), doi:10.1007/3-540-44467-X_10
8. O'Sullivan, B., Tibell, J.: Scalable i/o event handling for ghc. In: Proceedings of the Third ACM Haskell Symposium on Haskell, Haskell 2010, pp. 103–108. ACM, New York (2010)
9. Pyarali, I., Spivak, M., Cytron, R., Schmidt, D.C.: Evaluating and optimizing thread pool strategies for real-time corba. In: Proceedings of the 2001 ACM SIGPLAN Workshop on Optimization of Middleware and Distributed Systems, OM 2001, pp. 214–222. ACM, New York (2001)
10. Schmidt, D.C., Stal, M., Rohnert, H., Buschmann, F.: Pattern-Oriented Software Architecture. Patterns for Concurrent and Networked Objects, vol. 2. John Wiley & Sons (2000)
11. von Behren, R., Condit, J., Brewer, E.: Why events are a bad idea (for high-concurrency servers). In: Proceedings of HotOS IX (2003)
12. Willmann, P., Rixner, S., Cox, A.L.: An evaluation of network stack parallelization strategies in modern operating systems. In: Proceedings of the Annual conference on USENIX 2006 Annual Technical Conference, pp. 8–8. USENIX Association, Berkeley (2006)
13. Zhang, Y., Gill, C., Lu, C.: Real-time performance and middleware for multiprocessor and multicore linux platforms. In: 15th IEEE International Conference on Embedded and Real-Time Computing Systems and Applications, RTCSA 2009, pp. 437–446 (2009)

Non-intrusive Coscheduling
for General Purpose Operating Systems

Jan H. Schönherr, Bianca Lutz, and Jan Richling

Communication and Operating Systems Group
Technische Universität Berlin, Germany
{schnhrr,sowilo,richling}@cs.tu-berlin.de

Abstract. Coscheduling, invented originally on early parallel computer systems 30 years ago, provided the possibility to improve the resource utilization of these systems substantially by coordinating the execution of processes across multiple processors in time. Almost forgotten in the multicore era, recent research addressing certain problems on multicore systems, such as performance of virtual machines, contention of processor resources, or dynamic energy budget distribution, concludes that coscheduling is a viable solution.

In this paper, we do not focus on a specific problem or application of coscheduling, but on coscheduling itself. We present a coscheduling design that is able to cover most of the identified use cases on multicore systems and can be seamlessly integrated into currently used general purpose operating systems. We have applied this design to the Linux kernel and show that this approach allows a non-intrusive solution that fulfills the promises of coscheduling and is able to achieve a similar performance as a specialized commercial solution.

1 Introduction

Since the introduction of coscheduling by Ousterhout [1] in 1982, three decades have passed. Despite the potential of coscheduling or the stricter form gang scheduling defined by Feitelson and Rudolph [2] in 1990, it is practically non-existent in current general purpose operating systems. Coscheduling generally refers to the ability of an operating system to coordinate the execution of tasks in a parallel system, so that certain tasks are executed simultaneously. Correctly used, coscheduling is able to increase the resource utilization and observed performance of parallel computer systems for certain workloads.

Historically, coscheduling has been implemented on early parallel systems, such as the Connection Machine CM-5, the Cray T3E, and others. Here, it was mainly used to do coarse-grain context switching between parallel applications giving them the illusion of being the only program in the system. The benefits gained from this included efficient communication within the application and more and partly exclusive access to system resources (e. g., memory, I/O devices), while the operating system retained the ability to preempt the current job in favor of another one resulting in shorter response times.

V. Pankratius and M. Philippsen (Eds.): MSEPT 2012, LNCS 7303, pp. 66–77, 2012.
© Springer-Verlag Berlin Heidelberg 2012

Since then, the parallel computing landscape has changed substantially: multicore processors have reached the mass market including mobile systems and the server market is dominated by single- and multi-socket systems built from multicore processors. This development also caused a change regarding software. Instead of using operating systems and applications specifically designed for parallel systems, operating systems and applications from the single-core era have been adapted. Only now that multicore systems are ubiquitous, parallel programming slowly starts to become mainstream and many problems from clusters and early parallel computer systems surface again – though on different scales.

In today's multicore systems coscheduling can provide similar advantages for parallel applications by providing the guarantee of simultaneous execution, potentially simplifying the application's design, e. g., static load-balancing and busy waiting become valid design options [3,4], and allowing new designs to be applied in general applications, such as SMT helper threads [5,6]. Furthermore, access to certain resources, such as shared caches and memory bandwidth, becomes exclusive avoiding competition with other applications, increasing predictability, and (re-)enabling hardware specific optimizations [7]. Even workloads composed of sequential applications can benefit from coscheduling: scheduling applications with contrary resource demands simultaneously avoids contention [8], and the available energy budget shared by all cores of a processor can be optimized towards performance or energy-efficiency more easily [9].

In this paper, we present a non-intrusive coscheduler design that does not replace the scheduler of an operating system, but can be integrated into existing decentralized schedulers of general purpose operating systems. By reusing and rearranging their existing building blocks, our design keeps the important properties of the original schedulers intact: preemption rules, time slices, accounting, etc. It allows coscheduled and regular tasks to coexist without adding any peculiarities, yet it supports many of the identified use cases by providing a generic interface to specify groups of coscheduled tasks. We support these theses with a prototypical integration of coscheduling into the Linux kernel and an evaluation showing that our approach performs similar to a more specialized approach.

The remainder of this paper is structured as follows: In Section 2, we describe related research on coscheduling. Then, in Section 3, we present our design in detail. The integration of this design into the Linux kernel is subject of Section 4. Afterwards, the implementation is evaluated in Section 5. Finally, the paper is concluded in Section 6.

2   Related Work

In an early work on coscheduling, Feitelson and Rudolph describe Distributed Hierarchical Control [2], a full-fledged, gang-scheduling capable scheduler design. Similar to us, they use a hierarchical approach in order to realize gang-scheduling and to achieve scalability. However, their design stops short of supporting a wide variety of coscheduling variants as they had to deal with the shortcomings of the operating systems of that time. A variant of their design was later implemented on an IBM SP2 [10], a system with distributed memory. However, as distributed memory systems and clusters in general have to deal with increased latencies compared to shared memory systems, spontaneous coordinated context switches are either not possible or require some kind of hardware support.

Implicit Coscheduling [11], developed by Arpaci-Dusseau, relinquishes even the last bits of centralized control. Instead, coscheduling is realized as a side-effect of an especially crafted scheduling policy and waiting scheme that monitors communication. Together, a coscheduling of communicating processes is achieved. As explicit synchronization is avoided, the approach seems to scale well on clusters. Another implicit technique, Sorted Coscheduling [8], suggested by Merkel et al., aims at reducing the contention of shared processor resources. It distributes tasks with equal resource demands evenly across cores and uses a special scheduling policy that sorts tasks in a runqueue according to their expected resource demand. By sorting runqueues pairwise in opposite order and occasional synchronizations, tasks with contrary demands are scheduled simultaneously. The idea of implicitly realizing coscheduling has also a major drawback: these techniques cannot be used for anything outside their application domain. They cannot be combined with other approaches as they rely on a special task execution order. Similarly, they cannot be integrated into existing (non-coscheduling) schedulers.

An area where specialized coscheduling techniques are actually used today is virtualization: fully virtualized guest operating systems make use of spinlocks for low-level synchronization, which can considerably hurt performance if multiple SMP guests are executed concurrently without coordination. In fact, virtual machines can be seen as a special case of parallel programs with busy waiting. An advanced coscheduling capable scheduler is integrated into VMware's ESXi. It uses a relaxed coscheduling variant with special progress guarantees [12] blocking vCPUs if they advance too much. Similar to Ousterhout's coscheduling algorithms [1], simultaneous execution is only maximized but not guaranteed. However, being a hypervisor and not a general purpose operating system limits the area of application and restricts comparative measurements.

3 Non-intrusive Coscheduling

Contrary to other approaches, our design focuses on providing pure coscheduling functionality within existing operating system schedulers. We consider the following properties to be essential for our design:

Non-intrusiveness. The original scheduling behavior of the operating system scheduler – as observed from non-coscheduled tasks (or within a group of coscheduled tasks) – must not change, i.e., aspects like task priorities, preemption rules, or time slices must be preserved.

Versatility. The number of processor cores must be decoupled from the number of tasks to be coscheduled. Research on resource contention provides use cases where having more tasks than processors is useful (e.g., schedule as many tasks as possible from this group) as well as having more processors than tasks (e. g., schedule these tasks and avoid any interference).

Scalability. On larger systems, it must be possible to independently coschedule subsets of processors which may also differ in size. On the one hand, it does not always make sense to spread a parallel application over the whole machine due to limited speedup; on the other hand, certain resources (e. g., caches) are shared by only a subset of processor cores.

In order to be non-intrusive, we heavily rely on reusing data structures and algorithms already present in the operating system. The result of this research is therefore a design pattern or recipe. An actual implementation of this design consists mainly of managing and glue code. Our design is supposed to be applied to a decentralized scheduler with some kind of load balancing to distribute the work among all runqueues. For the remainder of this paper and without loss of generality we assume that these are per-CPU runqueues.

To decouple the number of tasks from the number of processor cores, we introduce the notion of a *coscheduled set*. A coscheduled set is a combination of a group of tasks and a possibly anonymous group of processor cores, where as many of its tasks as possible are executed by its processors simultaneously. That is, no core does something else while there are runnable but currently not executed tasks in the set. The decision which tasks should form coscheduled sets and the configuration of the available properties is left to some external component (or the user). This component is explicitly not in the scope of our current work.

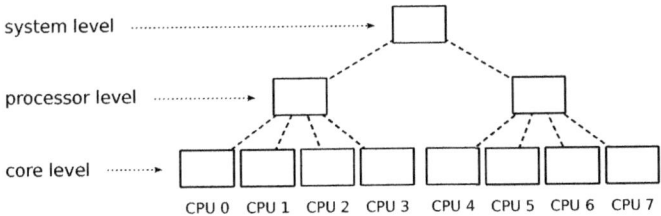

Fig. 1. Hierarchy of runqueues for a 2-socket quad-core system. The bottom level is equivalent to the already existing runqueues of the base operating system.

As we want to reuse the existing runqueue infrastructure, we need to generalize tasks to *scheduling entities (SEs)*, so that runqueues can also hold references to, e. g., coscheduled sets. Then, we introduce additional runqueues that represent larger fractions of the system and arrange them in a hierarchy which corresponds to the topology of the hardware itself. This arrangement is not chosen arbitrarily, but motivated by the different use cases given in Section 1. An example hierarchy for a 2-socket quad-core system is shown in Figure 1. At the lowest level, we have the original runqueues of the base operating system. The top-level runqueue covers the whole machine. If desired, an intermediate layer can be added if the

fan-out appears too large. Also, it is possible to omit some of the top or middle
levels, if coscheduled sets of these sizes are not needed.

A normal task is always enqueued in the lowest level of the hierarchy, whereas
a coscheduled set is enqueued at a position in the hierarchy that can accom-
modate it. This placement automatically maps concrete processor cores to the
set. Adjacent levels of the hierarchy are linked by enqueuing a special SE into
a runqueue, but only if at least one child runqueue is not empty. Additionally,
we represent every coscheduled set by its own set of (hierarchical) runqueues
as depicted in Figure 2. This allows an extensive reuse of the base operating
system's data structures and algorithms, which has some advantages: We have a
native support for more tasks than processors in a set. The original load balancing logic – adapted to work with changing sets of runqueues – is able to balance
tasks within a set and, when applied to higher levels, even multiple coscheduled
sets within the system. The possibility to nest coscheduled sets allows advanced
use cases, such as running SMT-enabled multicore VMs without any need to
explicitly bind vCPUs to host processor cores.

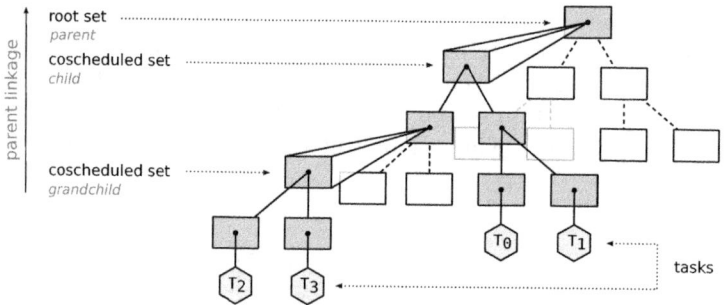

Fig. 2. Coscheduled sets are represented as runqueue hierarchies themselves

The original scheduling decision is also retained, but it is now applied recursively: with each selected SE we switch either to a different coscheduled set or to
the next level in the hierarchy until a task is found. For each position in the hierarchy of runqueues one processor is the *leader*. Only this processor is entitled to
make scheduling decisions within runqueues at that position. (Initially, default
leaders are setup during hierarchy creation, later other processors can take over
leadership if they need to preempt the current set.) Upon changing hierarchy
levels, the leader notifies the leaders of the direct children within the hierarchy,
which continue to traverse their part of the hierarchy in the same way. In the end,
the whole hierarchy has been traversed and every processor has found a task. This
basically results in the algorithm given in Listing 1, where `pick_next_entity()`
represents the original scheduling decision and `get_next_runqueue()` includes
the generation of notifications and modification of the `my_toplevel_rq` variables of other processors. As the synchronization is done only one-way and only
if necessary, different parts of the system are completely decoupled from each

```
task pick_task ( runqueue my_toplevel_rq ) {
    runqueue rq = my_toplevel_rq ;
    do {
            se = pick_next_entity (rq);
            rq = get_next_runqueue (se);
    } while(rq);
    return task_of (se);
}
```

Listing 1. Recursive scheduling decision within the hierarchy of runqueues

other unless there is a need to send out notifications, e. g., while there is no coscheduled set with runnable entities beside the root set, no notifications between any two processors will be sent. If a coscheduled set cannot occupy all its processors, some cores will reach an empty runqueue during their scheduling decision. Depending on the use case, this core should either stay idle to avoid interference with the set, or it is allowed to execute something else. In the latter case, the scheduling decision simply proceeds within the parent set. This way, no coscheduling constraints are violated: this set and the parent set are still coscheduled. (This especially covers all normal tasks which are enqueued in the root set.)

As our approach is designed to really guarantee coscheduling, it is subject to fragmentation issues which can be categorized as follows: (i) a coscheduled set requests a number of processors that is not directly supported by the hierarchy, (ii) a coscheduled set does not always occupy all its processors and allows them to execute something else, and (iii) it is theoretically impossible to fully utilize the system with the current workload of coscheduled sets without violating coscheduling constraints, e. g., a workload consisting of one large coscheduled set covering the whole system and one smaller set. The first category can be interpreted as a static variant of the second category. Nevertheless, in agreement with research on coscheduling use cases, we argue that constructing coscheduled sets based on hardware properties delivers the best results. The second category of fragmentation is caused by partially loaded sets. If allowed, idle processors can execute entities from the parent set – the only choice that does not violate coscheduling constraints. However, currently we can avoid costly search operations only when we select entities from a hierarchy level below that of the current set. And even then, we need some special load balancing rules to maximize the available choices. The third category cannot be addressed conceptually. We can only try to mitigate the situation by weakening our strict rules – for those sets that allow it – scheduling only a fragment, but it is unclear how such a set can be selected. We plan to address these issues in our future work.

4 Implementation in Linux

To prove the viability of our proposed design, we decided to do a non-intrusive integration of coscheduling into the standard Linux scheduler: the Completely

Fair Scheduler (CFS) [13]. The result is a working prototype on top of Linux 3.2 that is evaluated in Section 5. In this section, we highlight how the building blocks of the Linux scheduler were rearranged to realize our design.

Linux already provides us with the necessary means to handle groups of tasks: control groups (cgroups) provide a generic mechanism to partition tasks into hierarchical groups. These groups gain purpose by attaching one or more cgroup subsystems to them. Two of the various existing subsystems are of special interest to us: the cpu cgroup subsystem providing group based accounting via task groups, and the cpuset cgroup subsystem realizing CPU affinities on groups of tasks. Also, the concept of scheduling entities (SEs) is already implemented. A SE either represents a single task or, paired with another runqueue, a group of other SEs. A task group consists of one SE/runqueue pair per core. A group SE is enqueued in the runqueue of the parent task group for the same CPU only if its runqueue contains at least one (runnable) entity. To determine the next task to execute on a certain CPU, the scheduler traverses this hierarchy starting at the runqueue for that CPU within the root task group until it reaches a task. However, it is crucial to note that a task group does not constitute a schedulable entity as its per-core SEs are scheduled independently.

We use the existing task group mechanism as the basis for the runqueue hierarchy. Though, to keep the non-intrusive property, we must retain its original functionality of group based accounting. Therefore, we use the usual cgroup mechanisms to provide a per task group controllable flag indicating whether this task group should be coscheduled or not. Besides the original per runqueue SE that represents its runqueue in the context of the parent group and, thus, establishes inter-group linkage, we add a second per runqueue SE that implements intra-group linkage. When enqueued in its runqueue, it indicates runnable entities in at least one child runqueue. With this infrastructure at hand, we get two different types of task groups: *regular task groups* and *coscheduled task groups*. While the former resemble the original task group design extended to hierarchical runqueues, the latter constitute schedulable entities. Regular task groups do not establish any intra-group linkage; as with the original design, any nonempty runqueue is represented separately and scheduled independently. In contrast, coscheduled task groups are represented by their root node only, an adequately sized position within the runqueue hierarchy of a task group from which all enqueued SEs can be reached using intra-group linkage. An example of nested regular and coscheduled task groups and the resulting linkage is given in Figure 3. In addition, we modify the load balancer to gather balancing statistics not across all task groups, but per coscheduled task group (the root task group is also a coscheduled task group). This way, we achieve a balance within each simultaneously executed set of tasks.

In order to be able to specify a root node different from the top level for a coscheduled task group, we need the possibility to bind all tasks within the group to certain CPUs. This functionality is already provided by the cpuset cgroup subsystem via CPU sets. However, it requires to explicitly specify the allowed CPUs – a rather cumbersome interface for a user. Therefore, we introduced

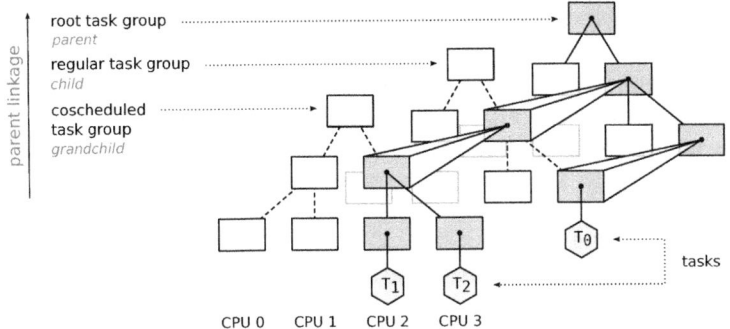

Fig. 3. Nested regular and coscheduled task groups

relocatable CPU sets, an extension to the cpuset cgroup subsystem, where only a quantity of CPUs has to be specified. The concrete placement within the system topology is done automatically along the hierarchy of runqueues, thereby modifying the root node of a coscheduled task group. Besides being easier to use, relocatable CPU sets have the advantage that the load balancer can move them around freely as the CPUs are now anonymous.

The combination of a coscheduled task group and a relocatable CPU set yields our sought-after *coscheduled set*.

5   Evaluation

The achievable benefits of coscheduling have been shown and evaluated elsewhere (e.g., [4, 8, 9]). Here, we concentrate on the coscheduling property itself and examine it in three parts: First, we briefly present results that indicate that our approach works as intended. Second, we compare its performance to that of a commercial specialized coscheduling implementation while we finally evaluate the claim of "non-intrusiveness".

5.1   Functional Tests

In order to show that our approach does indeed coschedule tasks, we ran some synthetic benchmarks and also used our prototype to realize some scenarios where coscheduling is known to be beneficial as described in Section 1. These practical tests included a set of experiments based on the NAS Parallel Benchmarks v3.3 [14], a virtualization scenario, and an experiment targeting energy-efficiency.

The synthetic benchmarks revealed that we effectively coschedule tasks in 99.98% of the time on our quad-core Core i7 860 (SMT and Turbo Boost disabled). In the remaining 0.02% not all processors within a coscheduled set participate because of context switches being not completely synchronous. Normally, a collective context switch is finished within $2\,\mu s$.

Some NAS benchmarks are sensitive to the available cache, others include a lot of synchronization. In an overcommitted system, these benchmarks profit from coscheduling: the former have exclusive access to the cache while they are running resulting in performance improvements of up to 30% in extreme cases; the latter experience no penalty for busy waiting and outperform non-coscheduled setups regardless of whether they use active or passive waiting. However, in many cases – depending on the benchmark, data set, and the hardware – coscheduling has neither good nor bad effects.

For fully loaded virtual SMP machines (setup outlined in Section 5.2), we observed that the performance without coscheduling heavily depends on how often the host "accidentally" coschedules the virtual CPUs, while experiments in coscheduled VMs have consistent execution times over multiple runs which are 8 to 30 times faster than in the non-coscheduled case.

Regarding energy-efficiency, we realized the method that we proposed in [9] by associating coscheduled sets with processor frequencies. This way, on processors with only one frequency domain, we can reserve the highest frequency for a few selected processes, while all others are executed at more energy efficient frequencies. The obtained results were very close to the predicted outcome.

5.2   Comparison to VMware ESXi

To the knowledge of the authors, VMware ESXi possesses the only production ready scheduler capable of coscheduling running on today's multicore systems. Therefore, it can be considered state-of-the-art. However, ESXi is not a general purpose operating system but a hypervisor. Hence, a comparison of our approach to ESXi has to be based on virtualization.

The workload considered in our evaluation is the parallel compilation of a Linux kernel (Linux 3.0) inside several guests in parallel. Disk I/O is mostly avoided by using RAM disks inside the VMs and enough physical memory in the host to avoid swapping. Our host machine is an Intel Core i7 860 (quad-core, 2.8 GHz, Turbo Boost and SMT disabled) with 8 GB RAM. We use either VMware ESXi 5.0.0-469512 or our implementation (based on Linux 3.2) with KVM 0.14.1. ESXi runs in its default configuration, while for our approach one coscheduled set with as many processors as vCPUs is created per VM.

We evaluate three different setups: In setup 1, we have 4 VMs with 1,536 MB and 4 vCPUs each. We compile the Linux kernel in each of the VMs at a parallelism degree of 8 to ensure mostly full utilization. Setup 2 cuts the VMs into half but doubles their number: 8 VMs with 768 MB and 2 vCPUs each and a parallelism of four. Finally, setup 3 targets partial load: We again use 8 VMs with 768 MB memory, but assign 4 vCPUs each and execute with a parallelism of only two. We do not use affinities inside the VMs so that the guests' task placement and load balancing are not affected. For each of these setups, we run an additional baseline experiment with just one VM and compare the actual performance of each case with the theoretical value achievable by simple bin-packing. This relative performance shows the overhead and effectiveness of the coscheduling implementation.

Table 1. Comparison of VMware ESXi and our approach

Setup	Approach	Absolute	Baseline	Relative
Setup 1 (4 quad-core VMs, full load)	VMware ESXi	354.7 s	90.6 s	102.1%
	cosched. KVM	382.6 s	94.7 s	99.0%
	vanilla KVM	9,697.5 s	93.4 s	3.9%
Setup 2 (8 dual-core VMs, full load)	VMware ESXi	716.8 s	176.3 s	98.4%
	cosched. KVM	756.9 s	180.7 s	95.5%
	vanilla KVM	1,208.8 s	180.6 s	59.8%
Setup 3 (8 quad-core VMs, half load)	VMware ESXi	868.2 s	173.4 s	79.9%
	cosched. KVM	1,484.0 s	175.7 s	47.4%
	vanilla KVM	1,723.7 s	175.9 s	40.8%

Table 1 shows the results and also includes measurements for KVM without coscheduling. After executing warm-up runs, the experiments show a deviation of significantly less than one percent between different runs (except for the vanilla KVM runs). Therefore, these results represent the average of the runtimes on all VMs and two runs after this warm-up phase. Considering only the absolute results, our approach performs worse than ESXi. However, much of this disadvantage is due to ESXi being faster out-of-the-box compared to Linux/KVM as the baseline experiments show. The relative values reveal that in case of a fully loaded system as in setup 1 and 2 our approach performs only slightly worse than the specialized ESXi scheduler. As the workload still contains some short sequential phases, ESXi is even able to achieve more than 100% relative performance by executing multiple partly loaded VMs in parallel – a feature that our prototypical implementation currently lacks. This limitation becomes significant when a partial load is enforced as in setup 3: our approach performs significantly worse than ESXi, but still better than vanilla Linux/KVM.

5.3 Non-intrusiveness

Finally, we want to evaluate our claim that a seamless integration of coscheduling into existing operating system schedulers is possible. So far, we focused on only one operating system: Linux. Therefore, we must be careful when generalizing. In particular, every implementation of our design is inherently unportable as it extensively reuses the existing infrastructure within an operating system. Similar to a design pattern, applying our design requires domain specific knowledge, resulting in a domain specific solution.

Our current Linux implementation extends the existing scheduler by nearly 2,000 lines of code (i.e., an increase of about 10%). Of these 2,000 lines are roughly: 20% comments, 50% new functions and data structures, and 30% additional code in already existing functions. Less than 100 lines of the original code were changed, i.e., coscheduling can be considered an add-on – at least in Linux. Furthermore, all major code paths within the scheduler remain intact. Our code just extends them instead of diverging from them, making it possible to retain most properties. Additionally, this simplifies porting to newer kernel versions. As an example, it took us less than 30 minutes to port our code from Linux 3.0 to Linux 3.2 despite a number of changes in the scheduler code (66 patches affecting more than 1,500 lines of code). From a source code point of view, we think that we succeeded in providing a non-intrusive implementation.

With respect to performance, we compared the baseline experiments of Section 5.2 using our kernel with similar runs using a vanilla kernel. As the baseline experiments only include one VM, they do not need coscheduling. In case of a fully loaded quad-core VMs, our modified kernel is 1.4% slower (94.7 s vs. 93.4 s), while for the other setups the difference is negligible (cf. Table 1). Stressing the scheduler with the messaging benchmark of perf (formerly known as hackbench) shows a performance drop of 2.1% (11.19 s vs. 10.96 s for 10,000 loops).

6   Conclusion

In this paper, we presented a novel approach to coscheduling that is not based on the idea of developing a new scheduler supporting coscheduling. Instead, it integrates coscheduling in a flexible and natural way into existing multicore schedulers. This approach does not only allow to retain major properties and most of the code of the original scheduler, but also allows to flexibly mix coscheduling with standard workloads. Moreover, for pure standard workloads the scheduler behaves exactly as the original one.

We implemented our approach within the Linux Completely Fair Scheduler as a proof of concept. This implementation runs stable and delivers a performance similar to the original CFS for standard workloads and a much better performance for parallel workloads benefiting from coscheduling. Furthermore, in virtualization scenarios it performs only slightly worse than a commercial specialized solution. The implementation is done non-intrusively, mainly extending the original scheduler code. This preserves the original properties and simplifies porting to newer versions.

While our results are very promising, some practical and theoretical issues still remain. On the one hand, there are scalability questions regarding our prototype. Albeit initial tests show that our implementation also works on larger NUMA systems, we have not yet done an in-depth evaluation. Then, we want to determine more exactly which use cases our design can support efficiently and which not. This includes the problem of fragmentation in case of partially loaded sets such as our setup 3 in Section 5.2 that we want to tackle at the design level. With respect to the applicability of our design, we are currently investigating other operating systems to support our claim of an operating system independent design.

In the long term, we also want to tackle the problem of forming coscheduled sets automatically. In this paper, we assume that this is done reasonably by applying knowledge of both, hardware and application properties. We want to investigate model driven approaches (existing ones as well as new ones) that consider these properties automatically and allow to derive mappings of tasks onto appropriate sets.

References

[1] Ousterhout, J.: Scheduling techniques for concurrent systems. In: Proceedings of the 3rd International Conference on Distributed Computing Systems (ICDCS 1982), pp. 22–30. IEEE Computer Society, Los Alamitos (1982)

[2] Feitelson, D.G., Rudolph, L.: Distributed hierarchical control for parallel processing. Computer 23(5), 65–77 (1990)

[3] Mattson, T.G., Sanders, B.A., Massingill, B.L.: Patterns for parallel programming. Addison-Wesley (2004)

[4] Feitelson, D.G., Rudolph, L.: Gang scheduling performance benefits for fine-grain synchronization. Journal of Parallel and Distributed Computing 16, 306–318 (1992)

[5] Kim, D., et al.: Physical experimentation with prefetching helper threads on Intel's hyper-threaded processors. In: Proceedings of the International Symposium on Code Generation and Optimization (CGO 2004), pp. 27–38. IEEE Computer Society, Los Alamitos (2004)

[6] Bulpin, J.R.: Operating system support for simultaneous multithreaded processors. University of Cambridge, Computer Laboratory, Cambridge, UK, Tech. Rep. UCAM-CL-TR-619 (February 2005)

[7] Datta, K., et al.: Stencil computation optimization and auto-tuning on state-of-the-art multicore architectures. In: Proceedings of the 2008 ACM/IEEE Conference on Supercomputing (SC 2008). IEEE, Piscataway (2008)

[8] Merkel, A., Stoess, J., Bellosa, F.: Resource-conscious scheduling for energy efficiency on multicore processors. In: Proceedings of the 5th European Conference on Computer Systems (EuroSys 2010), pp. 153–166. ACM Press, New York (2010)

[9] Schönherr, J.H., Richling, J., Werner, M., Mühl, G.: A scheduling approach for efficient utilization of hardware-driven frequency scaling. In: Workshop Proceedings of the 23rd International Conference on Architecture of Computing Systems (ARCS 2010), pp. 367–376. VDE Verlag, Berlin (2010)

[10] Franke, H., Pattnaik, P., Rudolph, L.: Gang scheduling for highly efficient, distributed multiprocessor systems. In: Proceedings of the 6th Symposium on the Frontiers of Massively Parallel Computation (FRONTIERS 1996), pp. 4–12. IEEE Computer Society, Los Alamitos (1996)

[11] Arpaci-Dusseau, A.C.: Implicit coscheduling: coordinated scheduling with implicit information in distributed systems. ACM Transactions on Computer Systems 19(3), 283–331 (2001)

[12] VMware, Inc., VMware vSphere: The CPU Scheduler in VMware ESX 4.1, white paper (2010)

[13] Giani, D., Vaddagiri, S., Zijlstra, P.: The Linux scheduler, today and looking forward. UpTimes 2008(2), 41–52 (2008)

[14] Jin, H., Frumkin, M., Yan, J.: The OpenMP implementation of NAS parallel benchmarks and its performance. NASA Ames Research Center, Moffett Field, CA, USA, Tech. Rep. NAS-99-011 (October 1999)

Automatic Parallelization
Using AutoFutures

Korbinian Molitorisz, Jochen Schimmel, and Frank Otto

Karlsruhe Institute of Technology
76128 Karlsruhe, Germany
{molitorisz,schimmel,frank.otto}@kit.edu

Abstract. Practically all new computer systems are parallel. The minds of the majority of software engineers are not, and most of existing source code is still sequential. Within only a few years, multicore processors changed the system landscape, but the competence to reengineer for computer systems of today is shared among a small community of software engineers.

In this paper we present AutoFuture, an approach that automatically identifies parallelizable locations in sequential source code and reengineers them for multicore. This approach demands minimal change to sequential source code. AutoFutures make parallel code easy to understand and increase the acceptance of parallel software.

1 Introduction

Parallelization is hard. After 10 years of multicore commodity systems, the vast majority of source code still is sequential. The knowledge about multicore software engineering is still shared among a small circle of software engineers. We see the necessity to address software engineers that do not have this knowledge.

[1] and [2] show that most of the time-consuming work is encapsulated in functions or methods. Critical path analysis methods also operate on statement blocks, so any automatic parallelization concept has to consider that the highest parallelization potential lies in statement blocks.

Automatic parallelization has the potential to make multicore systems available to software engineers of all competence levels. However, the parallelization process is still very time-consuming and skill-intensive. The most promising regions have to be located, the appropriate parallelization has to be identified and the parallel code has to be checked [3,4]. AutoFutures simplify and automate the manual parallelization process.

2 Scenario for Asynchronous Parallelization

To emphasize the necessity of our research we introduce a real-world scenario. Many real-world projects do not offer time for parallelization, so even semi-automatic approaches are too expensive. One way to gain performance boosts

V. Pankratius and M. Philippsen (Eds.): MSEPT 2012, LNCS 7303, pp. 78–81, 2012.
© Springer-Verlag Berlin Heidelberg 2012

on multicore systems are fast and fully automatic parallelization approaches. This defines the first mission of AutoFutures. At the same time, code correctness must be preserved. Because of these two constraints we can only use a small set of automatic parallelization techniques. Hence, evidently less performance gains can be achieved compared to dedicated parallelization.

AutoFutures' second mission is to achieve a broad acceptance of multicore programming in the target group. We see three flavors to accomplish this mission: Recognition, recurrence and correctness.

Recognition: As we face inexperienced engineers, we have to manage the parallelization process without their involvement. The software engineer must be able to directly recognize the parallelized code. Hence, our parallel code needs to be as similar to the original version as possible. The precondition for our parallelization concept is to be as unobtrusive as possible which naturally comes at the cost of lower speedup expectations. But to us any speedup is worthwhile when achieved without user interaction.

Recurrence: Another aspect to fulfill our mission to raise the acceptance is to use a well-defined set of recurring patterns. All parallel regions should follow a very small set of parallelization patterns. With this we lower the entry threshold among incompetent programmers. As we attain a higher recognition value we expect a rising acceptance rate.

Correctness: Parallel code that is faster but incorrect is preposterous. As this would lead to even lower acceptance rates concerning multicore programming, it is crucial to only parallelize where code correctness can be guaranteed. As a proof of concept, we implemented the pattern shown in figure 1.

3   AutoFutures: Automatic Asynchronous Method Calls

The first goal in our concept is to have an automatic parallelization technique that is very fast in execution. We use a static analysis to identify code that can be executed asynchronously. This precondition constraints the search space for parallelization potential down to code that can verifiably be executed in parallel without any data dependencies. This could be part of a compiler.

After code hotspots have been identified, we have to address synchronization. We make use of the widely known concept Future. A Future serves as a placeholder for the result of an asynchronous computation. Futures offer an easy way to specify asynchronicity and hide synchronization code.

Without a Future synchronization code has to be added at the end of concurrent activities. This breaks code readability and violates to be as unobtrusive as possible. Furthermore, Futures hide whether the result of a computation is already available or not. Figure 1 shows a simple example: Two consecutive methods *solve*() and *statements*() operate on different objects and do not have data dependencies. We suggest to transform the invocation of *solve*() using a Future. *statements*() is then executed in parallel to *solve*(). The variable x in the call to *print*() is an automatically added synchronization point, as the result of *solve*() has to be available here.

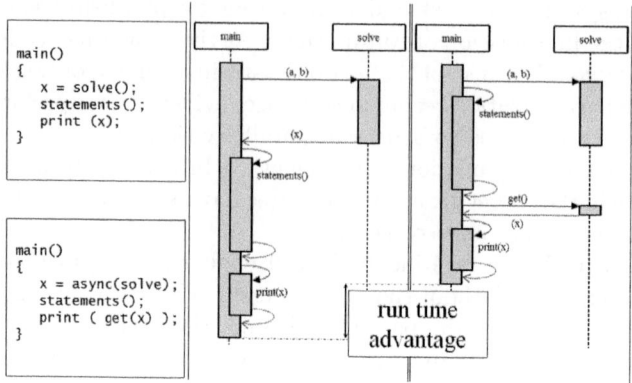

Fig. 1. Asynchronous method invocation

4   First Results

As a first experimental approach we implemented AutoFutures in Java. We base on the object-oriented paradigm so AutoFutures automatically convert synchronous method invocations to asynchronous Futures and insert synchronization points. Our implementation currently searches for the consecutive method invocation pattern shown in figure 1. We used the Soot framework [5] for the static analysis and developed two heuristics to detect the synchronization point.

Our key finding is that with AutoFutures we can detect parallel potential in sequential code and re-engineer it to parallel code with only little code changes. We evaluated our concept in 5 real-world applications and could achieve an average speedup of 1.81 (min: 0.76, max: 3.34) on an Intel Core2-Quad machine. In table 1 we present our results. In order for the parallel version of ImageJ to function properly, the store procedure had to be altered manually. PMD and ANTLR already run in parallel. We used the DaCapo-benchmark suite [6] and with AutoFutures we could almost reach the manual parallelization performance.

Table 1. Evaluation results for AutoFutures

	MergeSort	Matrix	PMD	ANTLR	ImageJ
Source lines	34	81	44782	36733	93899
Methods	3	5	3508	1998	4505
Input data	array	matrix	rules	files	images
Speedup min	2.16	2.61	—	—	1.74
Input size	1.600.000	400x400	—	—	512x512
Speedup max	2.70	3.34	0.91	0.76	2.04
Input size	8.000.000	600x600	13	18	1448x1448

5   Perspectives

We feel confirmed to investigate further patterns for the application of AutoFutures. Currently we conduct an empirical study to manually detect additional patterns in sequential source code by selecting programs from different application domains to explore applicability in different scenarios. This leads to an additional aspect: Efficiency. Not every parallelizable construct should effectively be parallelized. With the pattern approach we try to distinguish parallelization potential.

Our results so far reveal three additional patterns: Loop parallelization with and without in-order-execution, method extraction from blocks of statements and speculative value calculation as used in instruction-level parallelism. We consider extending our analysis method to include runtime information, as our static analysis leads to a very small search space. With the extension to include runtime information in our analysis the identification of design patterns comes into reach: We see the chance to extend the AutoFuture concept for the automatic detection of Master/Worker from sequential source code. The potential, limitations and tradeoffs for this approach need further research.

6   Conclusion

Although multicore systems are omnipresent software engineers are still afraid of parallelism. With systems becoming more and more complex we must address software engineers that don't have any knowledge about parallelization and don't have the time to learn.

In this paper we introduced the concept AutoFuture that enables a fully automatic code refactoring to help software engineers to familiarize with multicore software engineering. We argue that with AutoFutures the acceptance rate for multicore software engineering can be raised. Additionally, we see the potential to establish a parallelization process with variable granularity levels. For this reason it is possible to also address competent software engineers, provide them with more information and offer them higher speedup potentials. The free lunch might be over, but free snacks are still available.

References

1. Garcia, S., Jeon, D., Louie, C.M., Taylor, M.B.: Kremlin: rethinking and rebooting gprof for the multicore age. In: Proceedings of the 32nd PLDI (2011)
2. Benton, W.C.: Fast, effective program analysis for object-level parallelism. Ph.D. dissertation, University of Wisconsin at Madison (2008)
3. Tournavitis, G., Franke, B.: Semi-automatic extraction and exploitation of hierarchical pipeline parallelism using profiling information. In: Proceedings of the 19th PACT (2010)
4. Hammacher, C., Streit, K., Hack, S., Zeller, A.: Profiling java programs for parallelism. In: Proceedings of the 2nd IWMSE (2009)
5. http://www.sable.mcgill.ca/soot/
6. http://dacapobench.org/

Invasive Computing:
An Application Assisted
Resource Management Approach

Andreas Hollmann and Michael Gerndt

Technische Universität München
Department of Computer Science
Boltzmannstr. 3, 85748 Garching, Germany
{hollmann,gerndt}@in.tum.de

Abstract. Efficient use of computational resources is essential to get a high performance and a low energy consumption. The operating system (OS) is responsible for managing all system resources in a fair and efficient way. This complex task is, however, accomplished without having any notion about the characteristics of the running applications. The lack of information can cause severe performance degradations, especially on non-uniform memory access (NUMA) multicore architectures with their sensitivity to memory placement.

In this paper we present an approach how to augment applications with performance critical properties that can be used for optimizing the resource management within the OS or by user-level tools. We illustrate our concept using the OpenMP parallel programming model.

Keywords: resource management, resource awareness, numa, parallel programming, OpenMP.

1 Introduction

For computationally demanding applications the two most important resources are CPU cores and main memory. On uniform memory access (UMA) architectures and in particular for single socket systems is an efficient resource management rather simple compared to NUMA systems. The main memory is centralized on UMA machines and all CPU cores have the same distance to memory and share the bandwidth. NUMA systems have an integrated memory controller on each multicore processor, i.e. a NUMA node. This makes NUMA systems scalable without any change to the processor design, since the memory bandwidth increases with each multiprocessor added to a multi socket system. All multicore processors are interconnected and can access the memory on remote processors with a higher latency and a lower memory bandwidth. The NUMA architecture poses a new challenge for resource management, since it introduces a new degree of freedom, i. e. placement of memory. To make memory bound applications run efficiently it is necessary to use all available bandwidth, therefore, it is important to scatter the application's data to all NUMA nodes and additionally all application threads should only access data on the node they are running on.

V. Pankratius and M. Philippsen (Eds.): MSEPT 2012, LNCS 7303, pp. 82–85, 2012.

Applications are executed as processes with a linear uniform logical address space controlled by the memory management unit (MMU) within the CPU. This virtual memory abstraction fits quite well for UMA systems, but not for NUMA and its concept of local and remote memory. Applications are oblivious to NUMA and the resource management within the OS has only a very limited amount of information about running processes. These two factors result in an inefficient use of computational resources.

Linux, Solaris and other OS' use a lazy memory allocation scheme and physical memory is only allocated on the first memory access. This is also known as first-touch policy for physical memory allocations. The default memory policy in Linux enforces that memory is allocated on the NUMA node where the application thread is executed [1]. At the same time the default Linux affinity settings allow the process scheduler to move threads to remote nodes, reducing the memory bandwidth of this thread.

A way to control memory placement and preventing thread migration is to pin threads to CPU cores located at the local NUMA node before the first access to memory takes place, this is at application start. For parallel applications it is crucial to initialize all data in parallel using the same memory access pattern as in future parallel regions. This approach is, however, restricted to rather static applications. Adaptive algorithms have a changing degree of parallelism and data structures can grow and shrink during runtime. In such cases it would be beneficial to adjust the computational resources to the actual demands of the application. Additionally, information from the resource management system could be used within the application to adapt the degree of parallelism to the available resources in order to avoid oversubscription of CPU resources.

The above stated requirements motivated us to present a new resource management approach that focuses on strong interaction between applications and the resource management.

2   Invasive Computing

The idea of invasive computing [2] is to enable the programmer to write resource aware applications. In contrast to the overall trend in programming interfaces to provide more and more abstract or high level interfaces and to automatically map those to the hardware, the goal of invasive computing is to enable the programmer to carefully optimize his program for the available resources. This resource awareness comes in two forms. First, the program can allocate and free resources according to the amount of available parallelism or the dynamic size of the data. Second, it can adapt itself to the size of resources that are available for execution, for example, by selecting a different algorithm if less cores are available as were requested.

For each application we define a set of resources as claim consisting of CPU cores that are explicitly used by the application. A claim consists of at least one CPU core, but can grow and shrink under the control of the program and the system resource management. Two operations are defined for changing the amount of resources: invade and retreat.

The invade operation tries to allocate additional cores. Resource requests are specified as constraints, describing the amount of cores and their placement on the NUMA machine. Additional resources are only added to the application claim in the case of availability, otherwise an application has to continue with the already allocated resources. The retreat operation allows to reduce the number of cores in the claim. How many and which cores are released is again specified by constraints. Affinity of threads, i. e. pinning, is used for CPU core ownership and for placing threads to cores. The number of threads used within an OpenMP parallel region is also adjusted to the number of cores in the claim. In this way the number of OpenMP threads executing a parallel region is equal to the number of cores.

Resource awareness results in performance benefits for certain applications with predictable and repetitive memory access patterns, e. g. dense matrix multiplication. In applications that are executed in phases, which differ in resource requirements and scalability, resource awareness could be used to free resources in phases of low arithmetic density to be used in other applications. This means that invasive computing is a cooperative approach between different applications that improves the general resource efficiency. Another application area are adaptive algorithms, where the amount of computations changes during runtime.

2.1 Invasive OpenMP Example

Listing 1.1 shows the usage of the invasive computing interface. The application's claim consists of a single core when the application starts. In the initialization phase of an application there is in general only a limited amount of parallelism and no need for a big quantity of resources.

```
1  #include "invasive_computing.h"

3  int main() {
       Claim claim;
5      double a[1024], b[1024], c[1024];
    /* acquire resources according to the given constraints */
7      claim.invade(CPUQuantity(1,8), NUMA(scatter));
    /* executing a parallel for loop on the given resources */
9      #pragma omp parallel for
       for(int i=0; i < 1024; i++)
11        c[i] = a[i] + b[i];
    /* free resources, delete pinning after parallel region */
13     claim.retreat(1);
    /* continue application in with one thread */
15     ...    }
```

Listing 1.1. OpenMP example with invasive operations

Invasive API calls are inserted before parallel regions start. The invade method in line 7 modifies the claim according to defined constraints, CPUQuantity(1,8) and NUMA(scatter). These constraints specify the minimum and maximum amount of CPUs that should be used and the placing on the NUMA nodes. The actual claim is only known at runtime, depending on the number of running applications.

In line 9 the loop is parallelized with OpenMP. All resources inside the claim are used to speed up the execution. To be resource efficient it is necessary to identify the maximum scalability of each parallel region and take these numbers as input for CPUQuantity().

After the execution is finished the retreat method is called, which reduces the claim to only one CPU.

3 Conclusion

The introduction of affinity support in the OpenMP specification 3.1 shows that the resource management topic is of high interest not only in research, but also for parallel runtime systems that are widely used. In invasive computing we are proposing an approach that is more suitable for dynamic and adaptive applications, since we allow to trigger resource management interactions from within the application during runtime. The Linux kernel supports NUMA architectures since version 2.6, so they can handle memory allocations on different nodes. On the application side there is no support to improve the performance of applications, except the libnuma [3] library and its coarse grained memory migration support. In order to make dynamic parallel applications run efficiently on NUMA systems there are changes necessary within the kernel. In fact there were several attempts to integrate migration on next-touch into the kernel [4], but none managed to be accepted.

References

1. Terboven, C., Mey, D.A., Schmidl, D., Jin, H., Reichstein, T.: Data and Thread Affinity in OpenMP Programs. In: Proceedings of the 2008 Workshop on Memory Access on Future Processors, MAW 2008 (2008)
2. Teich, J., Henkel, J., Herkersdorf, A., Schmitt-Landsiedel, D., Schröder-Preikschat, W., Snelting, G.: Invasive Computing: An Overview. In: Multiprocessor System-on-Chip - Hardware Design and Tool Integration. Springer (2011)
3. Kleen, A.: A NUMA API for LINUX, Novell, Technical Linux Whitepaper (April 2005)
4. Lankes, S., Bierbaum, B., Bemmerl, T.: Affinity-On-Next-Touch: An Extension to the Linux Kernel for NUMA Architectures. In: Wyrzykowski, R., Dongarra, J., Karczewski, K., Wasniewski, J. (eds.) PPAM 2009. LNCS, vol. 6067, pp. 576–585. Springer, Heidelberg (2010)

Parallel Graph Transformations on Multicore Systems

Gábor Imre and Gergely Mezei

Budapest University of Technology and Economics,
Magyar Tudosok korutja 2. QB-207., Budapest, H-1117, Hungary
imre.gabesz@gmail.com, gmezei@aut.bme.hu
http://www.aut.bme.hu

Abstract. Graph transformations are frequently used for describing and manipulating models in model driven software development. There are several frameworks and solutions for graph transformations but in case of large, industrial-sized models, performance still remains a key issue. We are working on a transformation algorithm that can efficiently use the computational capabilities of the multicore processor architectures. By applying the transformations in parallel, our aim is to create a method useful in research and industrial projects as well. The introduced algorithm is not only a theoretical result; we have implemented and applied it on real-world industrial-sized models. The paper elaborates the test results and compares the performance of the parallel and the sequential execution. The results of the measurements are analyzed as well as future research directions are given.

1   Introduction

Usually, graph transformations are based on rewriting rules, where the rules consists of two main phases [1]. Firstly, in the *matching phase*, we search for an appropriate subgraph of the rule pattern in the model graph. Secondly, in the *rewriting phase* the match that was found is modified accordingly to the transformation. Most available model transformation tools execute these phases separately. The matching phase tends to be the bottleneck both in theoretical calculations and in practical measurements. This task is originated in the Isomorphic Subgraph Matching which is an NP complete problem [2].

In most of the available solutions, the matching phase means iterating through the elements of the pattern graph and searching for matching elements in the model graph satisfying all constraints. The order of the iteration is usually aided by a *search plan*, which strongly influences the performance of the execution [3].

The existing modeling tools use different optimization strategies, for example incremental pattern matching [4], or contracting common parts of different rules [1], or even runtime optimization of the search plan [3]. Although these strategies can effectively reduce the execution time of the transformation, the idea of parallel execution rarely appears [5].

V. Pankratius and M. Philippsen (Eds.): MSEPT 2012, LNCS 7303, pp. 86–89, 2012.

2 Towards Multi-core Transformations

Our parallel model transformation approach is implemented in the Visual Modeling and Transformation System (VMTS) [6]. VMTS is a graphical metamodeling framework which has built-in support for model transformations [7] [1].[1]

This paper introduces an improvement of the original transformation engine of VMTS, which was not able to optimize the execution on multicore systems. The solution can dynamically adapt to the number of cores in the processor to execute transformation rules in parallel.

2.1 Changes in the Transformation Engine

It should be emphasized that the parallel approach is not used instead of the existing optimization strategies, but beside of them. The algorithm consists of two phases: The multithreaded *matching phase* finds and aggregates all not overlapping matches in the model graph while the *modifier phase* executes the modifications sequentially, on a single thread. This cycle is repeated until there are no more matches. (The rules are executed exhaustively.)

The matching phase consists of three steps. In the first step the algorithm acquires a subset of all possible starting elements. This is done thread-safely which guaranties that each starting element will be processed by exactly one thread. The second step tries to complete the match starting with the pivot elements received. This step is not thread-safe, thus matches can contain elements which might have been modified by other threads meanwhile. The third step is reached when a complete match is found, otherwise the next pivot element is processed. In the third step the elements of the match are thread-safely rechecked against false matches, and the elements are locked to prevent overlapping modifications. The algorithm uses optimistic concurrency management: locks are placed only when a full match is found. The algorithm uses read-write locks: a node can be given several read-locks but only one write-lock exclusively. The lock itself is an integer given by a sequence that is increased when all possible matches are found in the original model. Note that rewrites are applied only after this, int the modifier phase. After a modifier phase the old locks become obsolete. New locks overwrite old locks, thus old locks are not required to be freed.

The algorithm seems to be very effective but does it raise error possibilities? (Deadlocks, overlapping or missing matches) *Runtime framework exceptions* cannot occur because the only modification in the parallel phase is the (int or long) lock-writing that is assumed to be atomic. Deadlocks are avoided by optimistic locking: no locks are placed until all of them can be placed. From two overlapping matches the accepted one will be the first reaching the third, recheck-and-lock step of matching phase; Hence we avoid *overlapping matches*. *Missing matches* cannot occur either, since the rules are executed exhaustively. Note that the

---

[1] The transformation engine of VMTS has produced the *fastest solution* in the performance case and thus won the Best Submitted Modeling Solution title at the 4th International Workshop on Graph-Based Tools: The Contest tool contest [8].

matching order is non-deterministic, thus the number of overall matches can vary. The efficiency of the approach is affected by the size and frequency of matches. There are some special matching structures where redex partitioning cannot be effective, however a good search plan can aid much. Effectiveness can also be reduced by recursive matches requiring a full search and modify cycle to generate the next match. But there is a notable performance gain if the quasi single-threaded parallel searching is the most significant part of the execution.

2.2   Testing the Approach

In our case study, the performance of the parallel algorithm was measured in transforming a model of YouTube videos. The paper [9] describes a *crawling bot* which downloads video data from YouTube website. In the first phase, the algorithm downloads the data of the most viewed, popular, etc. videos (180–200 elements); in the following phases it visits the first 20 related videos of each element visited in the previous phase. The depth of the tour is 4 or 5; a sum of 50,000–200,000 video data elements is downloaded, and a magnitude of 20 times more is referenced. In our research, a *VMTS model* was created and populated by this data. To compare the performance of the sequential and parallel algorithms, a few simple *search patterns* were constructed. The single-threaded algorithm does not contain any synchronization, nor does it have temporary match stores but executes the modifications as soon as the match is found. The parallel algorithm does take care of locking, storing, thread-safe modifications.

The **performance** of the parallel and the equivalent sequential algorithm was calculated in various scenarios. The algorithm executed an *exhaustive model transformation*: all possible transformations were realized until there were no more matches left. The main parameters to be altered were the *size of the model,* the *size* and *structure of the match* and the *number of threads* in the parallel algorithm. The measurements were calculated on a PC with Intel i5 CPU (3.3 GHz, 4 cores). Table 1 displays the parameters and the execution time of the chosen scenarios compared to sequential execution.

The results demonstrate that the *size* and *structure of the pattern* is the most important parameter in the execution. However, the *size of the model* is also important. The results display that such parallelization may be useful in various model transforming scenarios.

Table 1. Single Threaded and Parallel Execution Times

Match id.	Loaded Videos	Pattern		Avg seq. exec. [s]	Parallel exec. [%]			
		Size	Diameter		1 Th.	2 Th.	3 Th.	4 Th.
1	23,500	6	3	0.20	181.8	104.6	97.5	81.8
1	208,000	6	3	2.39	262.2	141.9	105.3	98.0
2	23,500	7	5	44.22	131.6	69.3	45.5	35.2
3	23,500	7	5	272.15	137.7	71.4	47.0	35.5

3   Conclusion and Future Work

The current state of our research clearly shows the potential of the parallel algorithm. In most of the cases, *parallel execution is already faster than the single-threaded*; however, in some cases it still needs further development. The goal of our current research is to execute *modifications in parallel* without having to suspend any running threads. Using *GPU-s* and *massive parallelization* also seems to be a promising direction. Although the size of the matching pattern is clearly connected to the performance, it is not sharply visible yet how the *structure* of the match affects execution time. *Synthetic models* would be also useful to generate various scenarios allowing orthogonal parameter analyzing. Moreover, *heuristics* could help to determine the scope of parallelization, which is essential for industrial use. Although there are several promising ways to improve the algorithm, the test results presented in the paper show clearly that the current algorithm can take the advantage of multicore processors.

Acknowledgements. This work is connected to the scientific program of the "Development of quality-oriented and harmonized R+D+I strategy and functional model at BME" project. This project is supported by the New Széchényi Plan (Project ID: T_AMOP-4.2.1/B-09/1/KMR-2010-0002).

References

1. Mészáros, T.: Supporting Model Animation Methods with Graph Transformation: Model Animation in Theory and Practice. Lambert Academic Publishing, Saarbrücken (2011); Ph.D. Thesis published as a book
2. Read, R.C., Corneil, D.G.: The graph isomorphism disease. Journal of Graph Theory (1977)
3. Veit Batz, G., Kroll, M., Geiß, R.: A First Experimental Evaluation of Search Plan Driven Graph Pattern Matching. In: Schürr, A., Nagl, M., Zündorf, A. (eds.) AGTIVE 2007. LNCS, vol. 5088, pp. 471–486. Springer, Heidelberg (2008)
4. Bergmann, G., Ráth, I., Varró, D.: Parallelization of graph transformation based on incremental pattern matching. In: Proceedings of the Eighth International Workshop on Graph Transformation and Visual Modeling Techniques (2009)
5. Boehm, P., Fonio, H.-R., Habel, A.: Amalgamation of graph transformations: A synchronization mechanism. J. Comput. Syst. Sci. (1987)
6. Lengyel, L., Levendovszky, T., Mezei, G., Forstner, B., Charaf, H.: Metamodel-based model transformation with aspect-oriented constraints. In: Proceedings of the International Workshop on Graph and Model Transformation (2005)
7. Asztalos, M., Ekler, P., Lengyel, L., Levendovszky, T.: Verification of model transformations to refactoring mobile social networks. In: Proceedings of the Fourth International Workshop on Graph-Based Tools (2010)
8. 4th International Workshop on Graph-Based Tools (2008),
   http://fots.ua.ac.be/events/grabats2008
9. Cheng, X., Dale, C., Liu, J.: Statistics and social network of youtube videos. In: 16th International Workshop Quality of Service, IWQoS 2008 (2008)

Reduction of Electronic Control Units in Electric Vehicles Using Multicore Technology

Georg Gut[1], Christian Allmann[2], Markus Schurius[2], and Karsten Schmidt[2]

[1] ForTISS GmbH, Munich, Germany
gut@fortiss.org
http://www.fortiss.org
[2] Audi Electronics Venture GmbH, Gaimersheim, Germany

Abstract. In the automotive domain the permanent increase in functionality led to a vast number of electronic control units (ECUs) in todays cars, but packaging and energy consumption became problematic in the last years. Thus it is vital to integrate more functions per ECU and shift in-car-networking complexity into software. To master this challenge, it is inevitable to use multicore ECUs, which provide more computation power with less energy consumption. We show how the automotive domain can benefit from multicore technology and how the software development model has to be addapted to master the newly introduced challenges.

Keywords: Multicore, Automotive, Software Architecture, Networking.

1 Introduction

The development of Electric Vehicles, in some facts, is a contradictory challenge that ought to combine customer expectations, quality and price. Thus, the redesign of these characteristics, going along with totally new approaches in vehicle characteristics, is indispensible for increasing the customer's benefit. The resulting layout criteria are not yet sustainably verified because of their mostly unknown, multi-variant interaction.

Therefore, the joint reearch project "e performance" is ment to demonstrate technical and economical feasibility on the basis of a re-usable module kit (a common base for vehicles classes "eCity", "eFamily" and "eSport" with different drive concepts). This module kit should allow to analyse and scale vehicle properties, the implementation over various vehicle categories as well as the mode of driving. This publicized, integrated development approach on the basis of "E-Modules" will be exemplarily demonstrated and evaluated using a collaborative vehicle concept called "e-tron research car 2012" [1,2].

One of the mentioned "E-Modules" on the car is the network architecture including the software components. The ever rising complexity of the historically grown architecture of nowadays cars leads to massive problems concerning reliability, costs and development time. The observable trend to electric cars offers the opportunity to redesign the information and communication technology (ICT) infrastructure of cars to solve these problems.

V. Pankratius and M. Philippsen (Eds.): MSEPT 2012, LNCS 7303, pp. 90–93, 2012.

2   Specific Characteristics of Electric Vehicles

The development of electric vehicles, seen as an alternative to cars with combustion engines, becomes more and more important due to rising gas prices and governmental funding. To cope with the difficulties involved, the development and introduction of a lot of new technologies is essential. Route- and cruising range prediction, adaption of charging times according to energy pricing, the energy store in the cloud as well as time and state dependent activation and deactivation of software functions are a few examples for this challenge.

3   ICT Infrastructure Goals

The permanent increase in functionality led to a vast number of electronic control units (ECUs) in todays cars, but packaging and energy consumption became problematic in the last years. Thus it is neccessary to not have a further increase and at best reduce the number of ECUs. Besides that and due to the the low energy density of batteries in comparison with gas the main objective in the development of electric vehicles is to save energy wherever possible. Hence this is a focus in the area of in-car-networking, especially as the functions needed for charging are spread over a lot of electronic control units (ECUs) and vehicle buses. Thus it is vital to shift in-car-networking complexity into software and integrate more functions per ECU. To master this challenge, more processing power is needed, which often comes with an increased power dissipation. To address this problem semiconductor companies came up with multicore ECUs, which provide more computation power with less energy consumption.

4   Use of Multicore Processors in the Automotive Industry

In the last years multicore processors have been introduced in the automotive sector. Besides their use in the Infotainment domain the main use case is currently to enable functional safety as required in ISO 26262 by means of redundancy at reasonable costs. Electric cars introduce new functionality which corresponds to several new hazards, i.e. electric shock due to malfunctions of the charging subsystem or incorrect torque output at the electric drives. Mature HW architectures like implemented in the E-Gas safety concept [4] covered safety integrity requirements up to ASIL D[1] by integrating an intelligent watchdog to monitor the main processor. From a SW point of view this solution results in a suboptimal strong coupling between application, monitoring and HW, thus negatively impacting SW development and integration. Consequently silicon vendors launched dualcore lock-step architectures in which dedicated HW continuously checks the status of execution logic between two identical processing elements. New multicore architectures allow trade-off designs between high safety integrity

---

[1] Automotive Safety Integrity Level.

and high performance through configurable lock-stepping on specific cores [5]. An example of a multicore processor that adresses the issues of the automotive domain is the Infineon TriCore family. Due to the combination of two different computation units (TriCore and PCP) in combination with a highly-configurable driver library for the Infineon TriCore family of devices it is possible to reach a safety integrity level up to ASIL D [3]. In order to deliver highest performance MCUs which also fulfil the increased demand for functional safety the newly Infineon TriCore AURIX is introduced. In this multicore architecture up to two of the three integrated TriCore processors are equipped with an additional checker core. Together with many dedicated protection and detection mechanisms this offers a very powerful and enhanced safety solution.

Further research is still necessary to exploit the full technical and economical potential of multicore technology. To reach this goal, the national research project ARAMiS[2] has been launched to provide the foundation for multicore enabled benefits in the transportation domains.

5   Software Development Process

The software development in the automotive industry is mostly conducted according to the "V-Model". Using multicore technology requires an extension to be able to handle the newly introduced challenges. Dependent on the location of a task, the runtime might change. Due to the fact, that RAM has less wait states than (un-cached) Flash, and Flash has less wait states than external memory, every task has memory dependent runtimes. Scheduling analysis on chip will become more complicated, with possibly different execution times on cores and communication overhead. Thus the left side of the software development model has to be adapted according to figure 1.

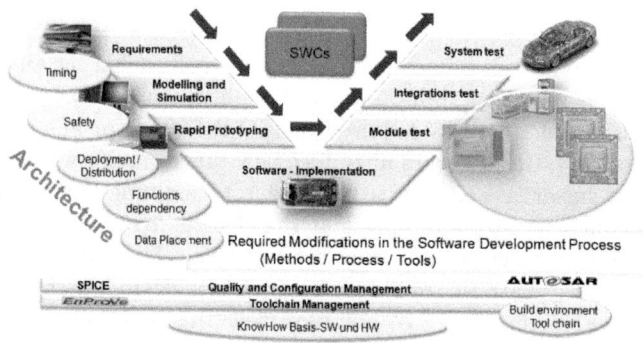

Fig. 1. Upgrading the development process

---

[2] Automotive, Railway and Avionic Multicore Systems.

6   Take Advantage of the Characteristics

Aside all these challenges there is also an advantage that can be derived out of the use of multicore processors in the automotive domain.

With highly integrationg SWC onto ECUs it is possible to reduce the total number of ECUs significantly. There are currently many discussions ongoing on how to group the SWC. Possibilities include grouping of SWC in a way to reduce communication demand between ECUs or such to reduce the latency between SWC by eliminating the communication over busses or by safety-level to reduce certification demand of lower safety-level SWC. Aside this goals on software and bus level, the superior goals on a vehicle-base is to save construction space and energy, which leads to indirect goals of less cabling, ECUs, weight and energy consumption of components and cabling.

A distinguishing feature of electric vehicles is the new state "Charging" (aside the state "Driving"). There are a lot of vehicle functions and thus SWC that are only needed exclusively in one them. We propose a partitioning SWC of both vehicle states, that are only active in exclusively one state, onto one same core of an ECU. For instance the control of the traction inverters and the charge management / charging device can be seen as a perfect use case. What comes as an extra benefit here is also, that all of these components need circuit points for integration in the high voltage network of the car. This leads to advantages for the cabling and thus also to reduction of weight and better packaging. This in turn can directly influence the energy consumption of the car in a positive way.

7   Conclusion

Our approach promises to help to reduce the number of ECUs, which - additionally combined with associated savings in cabling - leads to reduction of weight and thus to a possible reduction of the total energy consumption of the vehicle. This is valid for driving (due to reduced weight and less ECUs) as well as for charging (less ECUs that need to be powered).

References

1. Schüssler, M., Allmann, C., Hartmann, B.: Forschungsprojekt e performance. Aachener Kolloquium (2010)
2. Allmann, C., Schüssler, M.: Research Project e performance. Solar Summit, Freiburg (2010)
3. Brewerton, S., Schneider, R., Grosshauser, F.: Practical Use of AUTOSAR in Safety Critical Automotive Systems. SAE International Journal of Passenger Cars- Electronic and Electrical Systems 2(1), 249–257 (2009)
4. Arbeitskreis EGAS: Standardisiertes E-Gas-Überwachungskonzept für Motorsteuerungen von Otto- und Dieselmotoren, Version 3.0 (April 26, 2006)
5. Schneider, R., Brewerton, S., Eberhard, D.: Multicore vs Safety, SAE Technical Paper, doi: 10.4271/2010-01-0207

Author Index